# Pine Mountain Re-Views

## Stories by the Plumber's Daughter

by Lillian D. Champion

Pine Mountain Re-views
By Lillian D. Champion

The Chipley Historical Center of Pine Mountain, Inc.
P. O. Box 1055
Pine Mountain, Georgia 31822

# Foreword

One night this year at the monthly meeting of the Board of Directors of the Chipley Historical Center, those present were brainstorming about ideas for a new project for the Center. Malinda Brooks suggested publishing a book using some of Lillian Champion's previously-published newspaper articles and stories about Pine Mountain citizens, events and changes made in the town.

With enthusiasm, board members agreed and at the next meeting newspaper clippings, scrapbooks, and magazines with yellowed, deteriorating pages were examined. Photocopies were made of the available originals. Most of the stories were originally published in the 1960s.

Sally Sharpless, secretary for the Historical Center, and Elaine Bell, treasurer, volunteered to do the typing. When a copy was produced on Sally's computer, Malinda, Sally and Lillian met with a Columbus printer. Miz Rubye made suggestions, worked up an estimate, which the Board approved, and we were on our way to getting the book published.

We have written permission to use the stories from all the newspapers in which the original stories appeared. One story, discovered recently, was never published before. It is a rather humorous story about how Lillian became a writer. There is a little fiction in it, but most of it is true.

---------------------------❖---------------------------

*Update 2015: The Chipley Historical Center sold all of the original books printed and requests for more keep coming. The original publishing company, Quill Publishing, is no longer in business. So Malinda Brooks and Mary Ruth Mullins searched for another way to re-print the book. With a vote of the Board of Directors, they settled on reprinting the book through www.Amazon.com's www.createspace.com, an on demand publishing company.*

*Sally Sharpless still had most of the original manuscript. Malinda Brooks located all of the pictures included in the book. Mary Ruth Mullins typed what was missing; compiled the document and formatted it for publication. Ann Mullins and Malinda Brooks pitched in with proofreading. The cover is similar but slightly different, and there may be different page breaks on the interior. But the substance is still the same as the original book with some corrections.*

*These articles are reprinted exactly as they appeared in the newspapers in which they were originally published and use terms that have been discounted and which are no longer in use, but which were common at the time.*

*In publishing these articles, there is no intent to disparage, be insensitive, or to be hurtful to anyone. These articles and headlines are reprinted exactly as they appeared at the time in the interest of historical accuracy.*

# Table of Contents

# The Town of Chipley
Written in 1982

The charter for the city of Chipley was approved on December 9, 1882, and was signed by Gov. Alexander H. Stephens. Many of the residents of the town first lived at King's Gap and then at Old Hood, so let's go back for a few more historical facts about these two villages.

King's Gap was named for the man who operated an early hotel or commissary. A Mr. Jones had a trading post at the Gap in the year 1830. This fact is from a letter in possession of the Floyd family at Salem community which was written by John Floyd, urging his parents in the Carolinas to come south to the good farming country in this section of Georgia. John Floyd met Jones' pretty daughter at the trading post; later married her and homesteaded 200 acres in what is now Meriwether County north of Pine Mountain ridge.

According to Mr. Tobe Magruder, 88, present resident of Chipley, a leather tannery was in operation at King's Gap during the Civil War. Evidences of the tannery, ditches leading to vats in which hides were soaked and stones of foundations of buildings were discovered when construction of the picnic area of Roosevelt Park at the Gap began in 1936. There was a duck pond where the Liberty Bell pool is today.

The tannery was near the wagon shop owned and operated by Mr. Tobe's father, R. H. Magruder, who employed Crawford Key, a wheelwright from Alabama, to help him build wagons for the government during the war.

A furniture factory was among other businesses located at the Gap before the villagers moved to Old Hood upon construction of the railroad to the latter village site.

The man responsible for building the railroad from Columbus to Hood and to points northward at a later date was William Dudley Chipley. Mr. Chipley was born in Columbus, Ga., June 6, 1840. He was the son of Dr. William Stout Chipley and Elizabeth F. Chipley, the cousin of Col. Fannin who died in defense of the Alamo in 1836.

W.D. Chipley was educated at Kentucky Military Institute and Transylvania College. He enlisted in the 9th Kentucky Infantry during the War Between the States, and was wounded at Shiloh, again at Chickamauga, and was captured at Peachtree Creek.

After the termination of the War, Mr. Chipley settled in Columbus where he became prominent in the struggle to regain control of West Georgia. He was the first Chairman of the Democratic Executive Committee of Muscogee County. Arrested following the Ashburn Affair, in which a carpetbagger by the name of Ashburn was killed, Chipley was defended by the former vice president of the Confederacy, Alexander Stephens. The "Ashburn Affair" became such a sensation that it eventually led to the release of Mr. Chipley and to the withdrawal of Federal troops occupying West Georgia.

At one point in laying out the railroad, Mr. Chipley by-passed a small community, however, he did build a station to serve it and named it after himself. The former community was abandoned and a new community grew up around the station. Thus Hood moved to Chipley. A defect in the land title at Hood was one reason listed for building the station at the new location.

The town of Hood, located one mile south of the present city of Pine Mountain, was moved to the new station site (Chipley) in 1879. The land on which the business section and part of the residential area was built was a portion of the L. L. Hardy estate. The first residents of the new town were Layfields.

*Photograph courtesy of Lillian D. Champion*

**William Dudley Chipley**
**Railroad man for whom the town of**
**Chipley, Georgia was named in 1882.**

**He was born in Columbus, Georgia.**

The first businesses established in Chipley, including those that moved their stores from Old Hood, were Flournoy and Hunt, Layfield and Averette, Robert Spivey, Hogan and Phillips, Murrah Brothers, Moses and Wolfson, Bob Davis, Milton Jackson, Pitt Willingham, Storey and Taylor, Wiley Roberts, Jr., and E. F. McGee.

Dr. Quinton Purcel was the first postmaster and the first railroad agent was Marshall Dixon. The first hotel, located on the corner where Bird's Service Station is today, was operated by William Stripling. Another was operated by R. L. Magruder who brought furniture over from Chalybeate Springs. The first school building was a small two room house on the lower end of what is now McDougald Ave. The first teachers were T. L. Thomason and the Rev. S. D. Clements, a local Methodist preacher. Among the first physicians in the new town were Dr. Glass and Dr. Thompson.

The narrow gauge railroad built by W. D. Chipley from Columbus was constructed through Mulberry (formerly Kingsboro), Hamilton, Tip-Top (Summit), Old Hood and finally terminated at the new station, Chipley, until funds were available to complete the track on northward.

The train turned around at Chipley and went back to Columbus. The turntable for the engine was located on the spot where the former Dodge Motor Company was in business -- across from Tom Livingston Sr.'s residence. The first engine was the "Estes," the second "The Pine Mountain," and the third, the "Big 4." The track was changed to wide gauge in 1908. The old water tank, torn down in recent years, stood a short distance south of the depot.

The first church in the area was Bethany Baptist, established Sept. 8, 1828, with six charter members as follows: James Garrett, Levin Collins, Uriah Jones, Lucy Garrett, Catherine Simmons and Mary Jones. John W.

Cooper was the first paster. The Negro members of the church (slaves of plantation owners) were given letters of admission in order to establish their own church in 1885. As the town grew around the train station, a second white Baptist church was established within the city limits in Chipley. On April 30, 1887, a group of 37 members of Bethany asked for letters of dismission for the purpose of constituting a Baptist Church in Chipley. The names of these charter members of the new church are recorded in the minutes of Bethany Church.

Chipley Methodist Church was organized in 1882. The first pastor was S. D. Clements. The first layman elected as Sunday School Superintendent of the church was Taylor White.

Mr. Chipley later moved to Pensacola, Florida, and began developing a railroad to link west Florida and Atlantic ports. This railroad from Pensacola to Jacksonville is now a part of the Louisville and Nashville Railroad system. A town on the line was (and still is) named Chipley, Florida.

Mr. Chipley served as mayor of Pensacola, senator in the Florida legislature and on the board of trustees of colleges and universities. He died Dec. 1, 1897, in Washington, D.C., and is buried in Linwood Cemetery in Columbus, Ga.

A monument to William Dudley Chipley stands on the main street in Pensacola and bears this inscription: "Soldier - Statesman - Public Benefactor. On the battlefield he was without fear and without reproach. In the councils of state he was wise and sagacious and in his public and private benefactions he was ever alert and tireless.

"The history of his life is the history of the upbuilding of west Florida and its every material advancement for two decades, bears the impress of his genius and his labor."

The man for whom Chipley was named was a driving, dynamic builder responsible in large measure for the early growth of West Georgia and West Florida. For seventy years the movement of goods on the railroad brought livelihood to the little town of Chipley, Georgia.

-------------------------❖-------------------------

*Note by Mrs. Champion, 2008: The Rev. S. D. Clements mentioned above was the great-grandfather of Dr. Mack Clements, currently one of Pine Mountain's two doctors. W. D. Chipley's great-grandson, Dr. Lloyd Hudson of Columbus was on hand for the opening of the Chipley Historical Center in 1985.*

-------------------------❖-------------------------

**Chipley First Listed by Name in 1879**
*The Harris County Journal*, February 7, 1985

In my years of research on Chipley, both the town and the man for whom the town was named, the first mention of the village was in the very first volume of the Georgia Business and Planters Directory for the years 1879 and 1880. In the index of towns I found Goodman's Cross Roads with a notation -- "also known as Chipley." Goodman's Cross Roads in Harris County was established as a post office February 1879 with W. A. McGee as Postmaster, according to the information given in the directory.

Other facts listed are as follows: The North and South Railroad (also known as the Columbus and Rome Railroad) "will be extended to this point at an early date." The village was situated 8 miles north of Hamilton Courthouse, with cotton as the principal article of export. It has one steam saw mill, two churches -- Baptist and

Methodist -- and one school. Population about 300. Mail semi-weekly.

Names listed were: The Rev. Brannon, Methodist minister (he was pastor of Old Hopewell Church at that time) and the Rev. E. S. Harris, Baptist (he preached at Bethany Baptist during 1879 and 1880, according to Bethany's old records still intact).

J.A. Haralson was principal of the "Chipley School," and general stores were operated by B. Davis, George McGee, and Mark T. McGee. Calvin Hardy operated the saw mill. E.D. Hardy was the constable and John B. Hastey was listed as the justice.

Back in 1853, Goodman's Cross Roads was listed as a Harris County post office. William W. Goodman and James H. Huey served as postmasters before it was discontinued in 1859 or 1860. No further mention of that post office is made until 1879. Some believe that the railroad bed was first surveyed to run through Goodman's Cross Roads (Bethany Church area) en route to Rome via LaGrange. The route was later changed to run north toward Greenville and Atlanta.

The J.B. Hastey listed above was the Bethany church clerk. His "minutes" of church conferences before and after the Civil War appear in the old church records in his handwriting. He took time out to join the Confederate Army and was shot in the leg, necessitating amputation at Chickamauga on Sept. 20, 1863.

William Dudley Chipley, known as Dudley, was also a Confederate soldier. He, too, was wounded (in the thigh) that same day at Chickamauga. His close friend from Columbus was Captain Thomas E. Blanchard who fought in the same battle as did many others from this area of Georgia.

Earlier, 1st Lt. Chipley had been on leave and was in Columbus when Tom Blanchard was married to Sarah McDougald, daughter of Col. Alexander McDougald.

16

Another who probably attended the wedding was Elizabeth Ann Billups, daughter of a wealthy Russell County, Alabama, planter.

Those names sound familiar? They should -- since an early map of Chipley, Ga., lists Blanchard, McDougald and Billups Streets along with streets named LaGrange and Rome.

By the time Chipley was chartered on December 9, 1882, the little town was made up of people who had moved from King's Gap, Old Hood and Goodman's.

# "Miss Pauline" Presents Fiftieth Music Recital

*The Columbus Enquirer,* May 24, 1959

One of the most beloved citizens of Pine Mountain, Mrs. P. L. Hopkins, better known as "Miss Pauline," presented music students in a recital at the school auditorium for the fiftieth time last Friday.

She began her career as a music teacher in Chipley (now Pine Mountain) in 1909 with 33 students. Her first recital was held in May 1909, in the Chipley High School auditorium. Other members of the school faculty that year included Principal Bell, Miss Bessie Jenkins, Mrs. Lula Wisdom (Mrs. Tom Wisdom of Atlanta and Pine Mountain) and Miss Lillie Mann (who later married Dr. Jackson of Manchester).

Mrs. Hopkins, the former Miss Pauline Coart of Columbus, received her education in music at the Creighton School of Music in Columbus and at the Kidd – Key Conservatory, part of the North Texas Female College at Sherman, Texas. She chose the Texas college at the suggestion of an uncle residing in Texas at the time.

"Miss Pauline" married P. L. Hopkins in Chipley during the early years of her career. Except for a brief period when her children were quite young, she has taught continuously. A daughter, Polly, is married to a West Point graduate, Robert Murrah, and lives near San Francisco, Calif.

Granddaughter Molly is studying music and plays the violin. Molly's sister, Amanda, likes music but prefers to study art. Miss Pauline's son, Franklin, is with the U. S. Rubber Company in New York and he and his wife have three children, J. C., Pam and Frances.

"Miss Pauline" takes great pride in the accomplishments of her music students. Many have won honors in literary meets, some have played on radio and television and others used their talents overseas during World War II.

Among her former students are Paul Cadenhead, head of the current investigating committee in Georgia; Dr. John E. Champion, who is on the faculty of Florida State University at Tallahassee; Ida Askew Sullivan, who with her husband, the late Lt. Col. M. J. Sullivan, used her talents as a church organist in many Air Force bases in the United States.

Most of the residents of Pine Mountain were on hand for a surprise reception at the Woman's Club following the recital on Friday evening. Many of Mrs. Hopkins' former students were on hand to congratulate her and the entire town took part in presenting her with a silver tray as a token of their affection.

# Mrs. Hadaway's Dream Now True with College Degree

*The Columbus Enquirer,* January 27, 1959

To the casual reader, the name of Mrs. Russell Hadaway, Pine Mountain, appearing on the dean's list of LaGrange College students last quarter would merely mean just another bright student being recognized by the college.

But to Mrs. Hadaway's family and to the people in Pine Mountain it means much more. With her final examination papers completed last Thursday, Mrs. Hadaway fulfilled a goal she set for herself 23 years ago.

A 1936 graduate of Chipley High School, Mrs. Hadaway is the former Miss Bonnie Cornett, daughter of Mr. and Mrs. Otis Cornett, Sr. She was married to Russell Hadaway shortly after finishing high school.

Helping Russell with the City Cafe in Chipley and aiding him in looking after their farm out on the edge of town in addition to being a full time homemaker with three children, Bonnie kept rather busy for several years.

PTA, church activities, Scouts, civic organization, etc., filled up her spare time. In 1955, when her youngest child, Cecil, started to school, she, too, gathered up her books and went to school.

She enrolled in LaGrange College in Sept. 1955, and by taking courses through the summer from the University of Georgia extension school, completed her studies for her AB in Social Science at the close of the first quarter this school term.

Sometimes her schedule called for early morning classes. On those days she boarded the bus at 7:30 and got back home a little past noon. Other schedules kept her in LaGrange until 5 p.m. Encouraged by her husband, her parents, and children, she attended regularly.

Cecil, fourth grader, Charles, a freshman at Harris County High, and daughter, Carolyn, married last summer to Dale St. Gemme, Cape Girardeau, Mo., are very proud of their mother and her accomplishment.

Carolyn and Mrs. Hadaway were both students at LaGrange last year, the only mother and daughter team on the campus. Carolyn and her husband are enrolled in Southeast State College in Missouri this year to be near his parents.

Mrs. Hadaway did her practice teaching in LaGrange last quarter, where she taught history in the sophomore classes at LaGrange High school.

Her family, relatives and many of the citizens of Pine Mountain plan to be on hand when she receives her degree at the graduation exercises this June.

# Survey Team to Report on Pine Mountain Area

*The Columbus Enquirer*, February 3, 1959

Dr. Kenneth Wagner, head of the Georgia Tech industrial survey team, will make a report to the Pine Mountain Chamber of Commerce today on a community survey.

Dr. Wagner, and Dr. George Whitlatch, senior research scientist, will make their recommendations to the community at a 2 p.m. meeting in the conference room of the Gardens Motel.

The research team arrived in Pine Mountain Tuesday and made a tour of Pine Mountain with Mayor Earl Phillips and William Kimbrough, president of the Chamber.

A dinner for the research scientists and Chamber officials was held Tuesday at Callaway Gardens and then the Georgia Tech scientists met at a social gathering with Pine Mountain leaders at the home of Howard Callaway.

President Kimbrough has urged local business leaders to attend the meeting today and hear the recommendations of the Tech team.

Kimbrough said that the Chamber plans to "push the recommendations" of the survey team.

Business houses in Pine Mountain have already completed questionnaires and mailed them to the Tech team for study.

The survey being completed is similar to the one just completed in Columbus.

# Murder in Meriwether County

## Negro Found Dead At Fire Scene
*The Pine Mountain Review*, February 27, 1959

A fire destroying a barn at the G. F. Hall farm on the Atlanta highway a short distance from Pine Mountain, resulted in the death of Zollie Stinson, approximately 65, colored farm worker on the Hall farm.

It was reported that Zollie went out about 9 p.m. Sunday evening to investigate a disturbance caused by barking dogs and failed to return to the house he occupied on the Hall farm with his grandchildren. Around 1:00 a.m. Monday morning, Mr. Hall discovered the fire. At that time the barn was burned almost to the ground.

The body was discovered near a tractor in a shed adjoining the barn by Ed Dunlap, colored laborer on the farm, around 8:00 a.m.

Meriwether County coroner Wade Gilbert, J. L. Williams, justice of the peace, and Dr. Jack Whitworth of Greenville together with G. B. I. agent Marion Hale, made an investigation at the scene and speculated that Stinson apparently accidently ignited the barn from a match or cigarette and was sleeping or trapped at the time of the fire.

## Mystery Surrounds Murder of Meriwether Grist Miller
*The Columbus Enquirer*, July 28, 1959

*(The Columbus Enquirer's editor's note:  People of the town of Pine Mountain and surrounding areas of Harris, Troup and Meriwether Counties were shocked Thursday by the news of the fatal shooting of an 81-year-old miller. Enquirer Correspondent Mrs. Hubert Champion in this article tells circumstances surrounding G. Frank Hall Sr.'s death and comments of his relatives.)*

23

"I want the killer punished, but I want to be sure he is the right one," the son of G. Frank Hall Sr., said Monday.

The son of the 81 year old Meriwether County grist mill operator said he wanted the right person, but wanted to be sure it was the right person, because this was what his father would have wanted.

"Pop remembered when murderers were caught and killed in haste. Sometimes the wrong ones paid for the crime," the son said.

No arrests had been made as of Monday, Wade Gilbert, Meriwether coroner, said. He said enforcement officers are "working night and day" on the case.

The son, Ezra Hall, said that two thoughts dominated his father's mind Thursday morning. One was that the mill rock needed grinding and the other was a leak in the dam that needed to be repaired.

Although he had reached his 81st birthday in April, Hall was alert and agile. He insisted on doing quite a bit of work around the mill.

Ezra and his twin sister, Mrs. Betty Anderson, who is a graduate nurse, had both cautioned their father about going up and down the steep rocky path leading from the mill to the big white house on the hill where they have lived for the past 35 years.

"Pop, you have been too active to have to spend the rest of your life in a wheel chair," they said. Betty told him of cases she had nursed where elderly patients became invalids as a result of broken bones which healed slowly.

Thursday morning Ezra and Hall discussed the leak in the dam while Ezra loaded an order of meal for delivery into LaGrange.

The dam is built of rock which were cut and hauled to the site by slaves just about a hundred years ago. The rocks were laid with lime instead of concrete.

Every once in a while a hole would wash through the lime and Hall would plug it with a gunny sack or other material. He promised Ezra he would not try to repair the dam by himself but would wait until he returned from LaGrange so they could work on it together.

Just before the son left for his usual Thursday morning trip to LaGrange he gave Hall 12 dollar bills and two fives. Hall added them to the 15 ones he already had in his wallet. This made a total of 29 bills, which might have looked like a lot of money to anyone observing him making change for a customer.

Hall walked down to the mail box on the edge of the highway and picked up the mail. This was just a few minutes before 9 a.m. Ezra again cautioned his father about the rocky paths and left for LaGrange.

Just what happened after this is not clear. Hall usually opened the mail as soon as he got back to the mill. Thursday afternoon it was found unopened. If he walked up to the dam immediately after Ezra left he didn't intend to stay very long.

Perhaps he meant to open the water gate, let the water down enough to find the hole in the dam and just contemplate the repair job, as was his custom when he had a job ahead of him.

He probably meant to open his mail as soon as he got back to the mill.

The dam is about 500 yards above the mill. The wagon path is bordered by a thick undergrowth.

The water runs from the dam through an earth race until it reaches the metal race a short distance from the twenty foot water wheel.

One can reach the dam by walking in the earth race, but it is slippery. Hall most likely took the wagon trail.

His unknown assailant could have known that Ezra was in LaGrange and that Hall went up to the dam often to check the dam or to open the water gate. He could have seen what appeared to be a large amount of money in the wallet.

Hall probably was sitting on the dam thinking about the repair job when a single bullet struck the back of his head. This bullet came out just at the hairline on his forehead, according to the post mortem performed by Dr. Herman Jones, state toxicologist.

Death probably came instantly.

At 10 a.m. a Negro man came to the mill from Pine Mountain. After searching around the mill for Hall and failing to find him, he walked up towards the dam and walked up to the house and inquired as to the whereabouts of the miller.

Hall's daughter, Martha, told the man, Ed Dunlap, that her father was at the mill. After learning that Ed did not see Hall at the mill or near the dam, Martha went to a tenant house, which was under repair, and to other spots where he could usually be located on the farm.

He had not been seen at any of these places. Lunchtime came and he failed to come to the house. The daughter and others on the farm searched the wooded areas around the farm and then went to the dam.

They found his crumpled body. Dunlap stayed with the body and others ran to summon neighbors. Dr. W. P. Ellis, 79-year-old physician at Pine Mountain and friend of the Hall family, was summoned.

At first glance, it seemed that the elderly man might have had a stroke or a heart attack and had fallen. Blood on his face and running out his nose indicated that he might have struck his head.

Dr. Ellis was not satisfied that death was accidental and suggested calling the Meriwether County coroner and other officials.

It took a while to locate the authorities. The sheriff was out of the county. When Deputy Sheriff Joe Crews, Coroner Wade Gilbert, and county physician, Dr. Jack

Whitworth arrived, a shower of rain ruled out using bloodhounds.

Ezra Hall arrived home from his trip to LaGrange a short time after the body was discovered. After a few minutes of shock, someone suggested that he try to find out if Hall's wallet was still in his pocket.

The wallet and knife, which he always carried for whittling, were both missing.

## Murderer of Frank Hall Confesses
*The Pine Mountain Review*, August 7, 1959

Herring Davis, 40 year old Negro, admitted last week that he murdered Frank Hall, Sr. at Pine Mountain, July 23rd.

Davis had worked at Hall's mill the week before the slaying and had returned Monday and Tuesday seeking work there.

Pine Mountain citizens reported that Davis had purchased groceries and other goods for cash the afternoon the murder took place. ($37.00 had been stolen from the murder victim).

He was picked up a few hours after the body was discovered on the dam by members of the miller's family.

Sheriff Buddy Norris said that Davis confessed to the murder after submitting to a lie detector test last Wednesday afternoon in Atlanta.

Davis is also being held in connection with the death of Zollie Spence, a Negro laborer on the Hall farm, whose body was found in the ruins of a burned barn last February on the Hall property.

According to an unofficial report, Davis struck Spence in the head with a hammer, tied him to a tractor in a shed attached to the barn, poured gasoline around the area and set it afire.

Davis has been charged with first degree murder and robbery.

----------------------------❖----------------------------

*Mrs. Champion's note, 2008: Davis was tried for murder and given the death penalty. He was the last person from Meriwether County, Georgia, to be put to death by electrocution.*

# Chipley Doctor Helped Found
# First Georgia Pasteur Institute

*The Columbus Ledger-Enquirer Sunday Magazine*,
March 29, 1959

The carpenter helping me in remodeling the old Brawner home, in Salem Community near Pine Mountain, pulled back the last panel of sheet-rock for a final look at the six-inch, hand-planed boards on the wall of the "front bedroom" of the old house.

"Mrs. Champion," he said, "we're covering up a lot of history with these panels."

Just how old and how historical was unknown at the moment. My search for facts concerning the house and one of its former occupants, Dr. James Newton Brawner, Sr., was one of fascination to me and my family.

Ironically, word came of Dr. Brawner's death in Atlanta on March 7, just as I was organizing my notes for this story.

I have been corresponding with Dr. and Mrs. Brawner for several weeks and just a few days ago I received a letter saying that they were looking forward to reading the story with a great deal of pleasure.

We purchased the plantation from the Brawner family in the spring of 1945. From the dates recorded on the deed, it was purchased by James Middleton Brawner on Oct. 25, 1880, from A. J. Griggs. Mr. Griggs had been living in the house for several years, establishing the fact that the original portion of the house is nearly ninety years old.

Several of the elderly residents in the community recall that Mid Brawner first noticed the plantation while driving through the area in his buggy, headed for Smith's Mill in Troup County with a load of corn and wheat. He liked the "lay of the land" on the Griggs plantation adjoining the Salem Methodist camp meeting site, and, on his return trip from the gristmill stopped for a chat with Mr. Griggs who at the moment was repairing a fence between his

plantation on the West. Mr. Brawner expressed a desire to own the farm and with very little haggling over the fence an agreement was reached very quickly.

Shortly after this episode, Mid Brawner made a visit to relatives in Texas. His mother was a Ferguson, cousin of "Farmer Jim" Ferguson, elected later as governor of Texas. Ferguson and his wife, known as "Ma Ferguson" alternated as governors for a period of fifteen years.

Upon his return to Georgia, Mid moved his family, consisting of his wife, the former Miss Mary Buchanan of Harris County, and his four-year-old son, James Newton Brawner, into the newly purchased home in Troup County. Jim attended school in Salem and in Chipley, now Pine Mountain, and was known as an outstanding student. One of his schoolmates, 87-year-old Milligan Butts, resident of the Oak Grove Community very near Salem, recalls incidents taking place during their school days and told of a scuffle between young Jim and himself resulting in a broken arm for Milligan. For keeping the arm in traction, he was advised by Dr. Williams of Chipley to carry a heavy pressing iron dangling from his fingers all day for several days. Young Jim Brawner became interested in this treatment for broken bones.

He completed his high school education in Chipley and read medicine, which according to Mrs. Brawner, was a custom of that day, under Dr. Henry Slack, of LaGrange. In 1895, he entered the College of Physicians and Surgeons, in Baltimore, Maryland, now a part of the University of Maryland. He graduated with honors in April 1899 and went to Atlanta to practice medicine.

*Photograph courtesy of Lillian D. Champion*

**Dr. Albert Brawner, (third from left) born in Salem Community, 1893, shown at medical school.**

While taking a postgraduate course of study at the Maryland Medical College, he learned about the Pasteur treatment for the prevention of rabies, as developed at the Pasteur Institute in Paris, France.

He visited his parents at the family home in Salem at every opportunity and during one of these visits, a neighbor, T. C. Floyd, asked the young doctor to come over to his farm for a look at a horse which was acting very strange. Immediately, from the symptoms, the doctor suspected rabies and asked Mr. Floyd, who was also a relative of the Brawners, to keep a close watch on a pen of hogs nipped by the horse.

The horse died a short time later and Jim Brawner took Mr. Floyd's hammer and chisel and removed the brains from the horse for further study. Mr. Floyd's young sons, Theodore, Harry, Bob Frank and Edward Lee, all stood by while the doctor performed this operation. Three of the Floyd boys, now in their seventies, are neighbors of mine in Salem and recently told how Dr. Brawner made them wash their hands in a pan of water containing a small amount of carbolic acid after their observation.

The hogs died a few weeks later, following sudden illness, and the Floyds were convinced that rabies was the cause of the deaths.

Mr. Bob Frank said that a few goats were also nipped by the mad horse but escaped the disease because their tough hides were not broken.

After completing his postgraduate course, Dr. Brawner went to Europe at the insistence of Dr. Slack and visited the Pasteur Institute.

When he returned to his parents' home in Salem, from France, he brought with him a number of white rabbits, some inoculated with rabies. He prepared his serum for the rabies treatment from the inoculated rabbits. Lacking a refrigerator, he dug a hole under the house (underneath my bedroom today) and placed the bottles of serum in the hole containing ice brought from either LaGrange or Chipley.

The Floyd boys and Mr. Milligan Butts vividly recall the experiments with the animals. They watched while the young doctor injected the rabies germ into two dogs and several rabbits. They were present when Dr. Jim performed an "autopsy" on the dog, which he allowed to die. He saved the other one. The dead rabbits and dog were buried by Negroes on the farm. He cured some of the infected rabbits and used them to prepare more serum.

Always, Dr. Jim used carbolic acid and water as a disinfectant after his experiments, and made the young boys wash their hands thoroughly even though they watched from a distance.

Mr. Bob Frank Floyd credited Dr. Jim with the distinction of owning the first bicycle in Salem, which interested the young Floyd boys almost as much as the experiments with the animals.

In 1900, he left the farm in Salem, satisfied with his experiments, and established the Georgia Pasteur Institute in Atlanta, using serum prepared from his rabbits. This Institute was the FIRST of its kind in the South. Patients from every southern state were treated there by Dr. Brawner until the State of Georgia established free treatment for the prevention of rabies a few years later. The State of Georgia developed its serum from inoculated rabbits given by Dr. Brawner. (This information comes from one of the letters I received very recently from Dr. and Mrs. Brawner.)

After closing the Institute, Dr. Brawner opened the Brawner Sanitarium in Smyrna on September 1, 1910, for the treatment of nervous and mental diseases and alcoholism. He retired from active practice about four years ago and the hospital is now under the management of his son, Dr. James N. Brawner, Jr., a graduate of Johns

Hopkins, and his brother Dr. Albert Brawner, who was born in my house in Salem in 1890.

Mrs. Brawner wrote that Dr. Brawner had been an invalid for a couple of years and that my snapshots of the old home place brought back many memories.

Dr. and Mrs. Brawner, the former Miss Nellie V. Barksdale, daughter of Charles Edward and Cynthia M. Barksdale, were married in 1902 and were the parents of five children, two of whom are deceased. Dr. James Newton Brawner, Jr., Charles M. Brawner, and Mrs. David E. Miller reside in Atlanta. A grandson, James N. Brawner 3rd, will graduate from Johns Hopkins after one more year of study.

Dr. Brawner, Sr. has served as president of the Fulton County Medical Society, 1930, as a member of the Atlanta Board of Health, and was a member of the Georgia and Southern Psychiatric Associations. He is the author of a book, "The Mind and Its Disorders" and numerous articles on medical subjects, widely used in Medical schools and among the profession.

I did not have the pleasure of meeting Dr. Brawner personally, but I feel as though I knew him. The childish initials carved on the door facing at the rear of old house were those of Jim and Albert Brawner. So many things I see around the old house and the farm must have been familiar sights to him during his childhood. He would have enjoyed seeing the lake built in recent years on the spot where once stood the old springhouse for the "camp meeting" sessions. The house, like Topsy, has "growed". The original was a stout, firm structure built of "heart pine," four rooms and a hall. Years later, two more rooms and another hall were added. Today, we have eight rooms and all the modern conveniences; a far cry from the plantation life of Dr. Brawner's early childhood.

Many have asked why we didn't tear down the old house and start anew, instead of struggling through all the problems involved in modernizing. Like the proverbial old shoe, we find it very comfortable and we hope that some of the good luck for success will rub off on the present four occupants, each striving for different goals, one as a dairyman, one as a small-scale news writer, another as a future scientist and another, not quite adolescent, whose ambitions change from day to day.

*Note by Mrs. Champion, 2008: A few years ago Louis Floyd, son of Harry Floyd, found a copy of Dr. Brawner's book at a yard sale. Mrs. Champion's son, Richard M. Champion, who grew up in the Brawner house, is a physician in Birmingham in 2008.*

# William Phelps Ellis, M.D.

**Dr. W. P. Ellis Honored for 53 Years Service**
*The Columbus Enquirer*, June 12, 1959

A "This is Your Life" program and reception honoring Dr. W. P. Ellis of Pine Mountain was held Sunday afternoon, June 7th, at 4:00 p.m. at the High School Gymnasium in Hamilton.

A capacity crowd, estimated at more than 600 persons, filled the gym to overflowing.

The program and reception were planned by citizens of Harris County to express appreciation to the beloved doctor, who will be eighty years old in October and has served in the medical profession at Gay and Pine Mountain for a total of 53 years.

Dr. William Chambless of Pine Mt. Valley was general chairman of the occasion. Dr. Joe Miller, Manchester, (native of Chipley) served as master of ceremonies.

The program depicted important events in the life of Dr. Ellis. Warren Patrick, dressed in the fashion of 1906, portrayed the doctor at medical school. Hoke Askew, Pine Mt., played the part of the doctor as a captain in the Medical Corps in 1918.

The "roaring Twenties" was depicted with a Charleston by Meda Miller of Manchester and appropriate songs by a quartet composed of Mrs. Milton Rexrode, Mrs. Ken Askew, Delton Hoxsie and Forest Salter. The audience joined in signing, with Miss Gertrude Handley and her orchestra providing the music. Jesse McGee told about the doctor's hobby -- fishing.

*Photograph courtesy of Minnie Ellis Whitaker*

**William P. Ellis, M.D.**

A parade of "babies" delivered through the years by Dr. Ellis was led across the stage in front of the doctor by Imogene Huling, Dr. Ellis' first Harris Co. baby. The doctor's very first baby, Jim Henry Drew of Gay was also present. He was born in Gay in July 1906, shortly after the doctor began his practice in Meriwether County. Mr. Drew's parents were also present.

Gifts were presented by Dr. V. H. Bennett, Dr. Ellis' one-time partner at Gay and by B. W. Williams of Hamilton in behalf of the citizens of Gay and Harris County and the surrounding communities.

Included in the gifts were a recording machine and a subscription of tapes from the Medical Journal, also a leather bound volume of letters from friends, former patients and "babies" of the physician.

Following the program an informal reception was held at the gymnasium. Cookies, punch and ice cream were served.

The doctor's family, his sisters, children and grandchildren were on hand for the occasion, which was a surprise to Dr. Ellis.

Dr. Ellis was born on October 22, 1879, at Oakland, Meriwether Co., one of the five children of Davenport Phelps Ellis and Lucy Atkinson Ellis. The other children included Lucy A. Ellis (Mrs. R. G. Ross), Misses Mae A. Ellis and Dora A. Ellis who reside in Charlotte, N.C., and Leroy R. Ellis, deceased.

The mother was a graduate of Vassar College, and was most interested in the education of her children.

Young Ellis attended Oakland public school and later Jackson High School at Jackson, Ga., while living with an aunt, Mrs. Marcus W. Beck, whose husband was serving in the Spanish-American War at the time. Mrs. Beck, now 97 years of age, lives in St. Mary, Ga., today.

He graduated from Gordon Military Institute in 1901 with honors, after the family had moved to Barnesville.

He was anxious to study medicine, but finances were limited with the other children to be educated, too, so he went to work in the summer with a kinsman, Dr. R. A. Mallory, Concord, Ga., in order to help finance his schooling.

In the fall he taught school in Gay and the following summer worked at the famous Meriwether Inn at Warm Springs. His job there consisted of answering calls from the desk, anything from shining shoes to driving the surrey to the depot to meet incoming guests arriving on the train. The surrey he drove is the one on exhibit in the museum at the Little White House.

With odd jobs and the help of a relative who made him a loan, he finished his study and graduated from the Atlanta Medical School (now Emory University) in 1906 and bought the necessary instruments to begin his practice.

He used a horse and buggy to cover the area around Gay until he purchased one of the first autos in the county in 1909.

In 1911, he took on a partner, Dr. V. H. Bennett from Commerce, Ga., and the two young doctors operated the first drug store in that part of the county in addition to their duties as physicians. Miss. Maude Cole managed the drug store and purchased it when Dr. Ellis moved to Chipley.

Dr. Ellis was married to Miss Bertha Mae Abshire from Kalamazoo, Mich., in 1915. She was a registered nurse and shared his work until her death in 1943. They were the parents of four children, Leroy R. W. Y., Theodore R., and Minnie A. (Mrs. J. G. Whitaker, Columbus, Ga.). Leroy died in 1950. There are seven grandchildren.

He volunteered for active service in the Medical Corps in 1917 and served overseas from May 1918 to June 1919. He was promoted to the rank of Captain.

After returning to his practice in Gay, he and Dr. Bennett continued their partnership until 1929, when they learned that Drs. Archer, Parham, and Williams were all leaving or retiring from practice at Chipley. He and Dr. Bennett tossed a coin to decide which one should move to Chipley.

A short time after he came to Chipley he employed Ernestine Surles as receptionist, bookkeeper and assistant nurse. Mrs. Surles has served in this capacity for 28 years.

Dr. Ellis served as physician for the boys of the Civilian Conservation Corps, Harris County Public Health Dept., and the Harris Co. Selective Service Board. He received a pin for 50 years of professional service from the Ga. Medical Association in 1956 and a 25 year pin from the Central of Ga. Railroad as Surgeon Emeritus.

Other public offices include Board of Education, Meriwether Co., 1926-1929, City Councilman in Chipley, and held clinics in Pine Mt. Valley in the early stages of its development.

He and the former Mrs. Elsie Smith O'Neal, who held the office of ordinary at Greenville for many years, were married in 1948. She plans his office hours and home visits during the mornings so he can have the afternoons free to enjoy his hobby -- fishing.


**That Fishing Doctor from Pine Mountain**
*The Columbus Ledger-Enquirer Sunday Magazine*, October 23, 1960

In Pine Mountain, Ga., this notice appears quite frequently on the office door of the town's only medical doctor:

"The Good Lord made six times as much water as He did dry land, so as any fool can plainly see, He meant for man to fish six times as much as he works."

The remarkable physician who follows this rule has apparently found the secret of long life and happiness. He is Dr. William Phelps Ellis, and he observed his 81st birthday yesterday, Oct. 22.

His daily routine calls for holding office hours in the morning and fishing in the afternoon. Citizens of the town and residents of communities throughout Harris and surrounding counties are perfectly satisfied with the arrangement -- they feel that a man who has served the medical profession faithfully for 54 years deserves to go fishing as often as he pleases.

A native of Gay, Ga., the doctor began his practice in Meriwether County in 1906. He moved to Chipley (now Pine Mountain) in 1929 and has been the town's only doctor for most of the 31 years since.

Last year a "Dr. Ellis Day" was held in Harris County and messages of love and congratulations poured in from people in every walk of life. A lifetime of service to humanity is reflected in these letters written by former patients, babies he delivered (now adults) and just plain friends, who number in the thousands.

A prominent LaGrange physician wrote, "One of my earliest recollections was the drawing up of a petition by the people in my community of Gay, Ga., urging you to stay in Gay.

"Of Course, your plans had already been made, and one community's loss was another's gain. When I came to LaGrange to practice medicine, I soon learned that your diagnostic acumen had become legendary in this area. It very quickly became obvious that you were held in the highest esteem, both for your medical ability and your integrity as a person."

Another LaGrange doctor said, "There are many impressions that I have formed about Dr. Ellis over the years. One is his devotion to the sick and to his community; another has been his absolute honesty with his patients, which I think is the greatest tribute that can be paid to a doctor.

"Another impression is that he is about the most conscientious Wednesday afternoon fisherman that I have ever known, and I also think he is about as good a spring lizard fisherman as there is in the state -- even though he occasionally lets a big one get away."

Dr. Ellis has probably received more invitations to fish in private lakes than any person in this section of Georgia. One of his "babies" invited him in this manner:

"As one fisherman to another, I want to say thank you for bringing me to the family you did, since they saw fit to build me a great big lake. I want you to know that the fish are jumping in 'Penny's Pond' and any day you would like to come, just drive up and help yourself."

A former patient, now residing in another state, expressed her thoughts about the doctor's love for fishing in the following note: "It seems to say that here is a man who recognizes a need to relax mind, body and soul. I have always admired him for taking time to appreciate and enjoy the simple gifts of nature that so many take for granted."

"I remember Dr. Ellis," wrote a former Pine Mountain resident now living in a distant state. "I remember kicking him in the stomach once when he mopped my throat. Of course, I was a small child. Later I remember the look of compassion on his face when he came to tell my mother that my father had died of a heart attack on a fishing trip. Some people remember a doctor's hands, but it is always his face that I remember."

On Nov. 16, 1931, Dr. Ellis delivered the first of 10 children born to a family at Blue Springs in Harris County.

The baby, a girl, weighed only a pound and one-half, and, to the surprise of her parents and the doctor, she lived and had a happy, healthy childhood. A recent letter from the miracle baby, now married, declared, "Dr. Ellis is the most outstanding doctor I have ever known."

Wrote a Pine Mountain teen-ager: "It should give you great joy and pride just to know you brought me here April 18, 1945. I'm tickled to death myself, but I understand mother cried all night. They already had one girl."

Another teenager said, "Thanks for hurrying up your cure for the Junior-Senior Prom. I would have hated to have missed it."

The winner in a recent county election told the fishing physician: "Although I had nothing to do with it, I am very proud to be one of your children. I am sorry to have kept you waiting, however. I am sure that working in the garden kept you from just waiting around." This extraordinary baby grew up to be Harris County's ordinary.

Testifying to Dr. Ellis' great heart was a former patient who said, "I was ill for three years. I stayed down so long that my money gave out. Dr. Ellis knew that I couldn't pay and yet he continued to see me daily."

A specialist in a neighboring county wrote, "I remember cases he brought to the hospital in his own car because there was no other means of transportation. I also can remember cases not eligible for charity, yet unable to pay for a hospital bill, for whom he underwrote expenses. I know of many instances when he made home calls on muddy, slick and freezing roads at night when I know he actually felt worse than the patient he was going to see."

The doctor added: "His continued reading and studying of current medical literature in the desire and need to keep up with all of the latest knowledge in medical science has been an inspiration to me and to many other doctors in the area."

A letter from the office of Senator Herman Talmadge stated, "Your more than 50 years of active service as a physician is a record that few men achieve. I want to add my congratulations to those you have already received."

The small fry also commented on their favorite doctor: "Your needles look wicked, but YOU are nice." "He gave me a nickel 'cause I'm a big girl and I didn't cry." "Roses are red, violets are blue, your lollipops are sweet, and so are you."

Among the letters in the bound volume which was presented to Dr. Ellis on the day of the countywide recognition service are many personal messages from patient to doctor, friend to fellow fisherman and from boyhood chums and school classmates.

Also contributing to the "Festschrift" or feast of words for the "Dr. Ellis Book" were the State Department of Public Health, various state and county organizations, pharmaceutical establishments, and professional associates of his long years of practice.

Perhaps the most touching tribute came from a Columbus physician who said, "One of the most difficult tasks that comes to any physician is the care of the dying. It is also the role in which the physician is often seen at his best.

"It was in this setting that I really came to know Dr. Ellis. His tenderness, compassion, gentleness, humility and devotion to duty were personal qualities that came sharply into focus as I saw him caring for a patient who was also his good friend.

"As I looked through the window and saw him administering drugs to relieve her pain, I had the sensation that I had seen a living picture of the art of medicine at its highest and best."

Thus the sentiments of about half the population of Harris County can be summed up as follows:

"Enjoy the richness of your golden years, Dr. Ellis, but keep up the fishing because you enjoy it so much. May the bait be good, the line be strong and may the fish keep biting. And may God bless you."

## Dr. W. P. Ellis Passes Away
*The Pine Mountain Review*, December 22, 1966

Dr. William Phelps Ellis, 87, one of Harris County's most beloved citizens, died at 8:40 a.m., Friday, December 16, at The Medical Center in Columbus, following a long illness.

Survivors include four daughters, Mrs. John G. Whitaker, Columbus; Mrs. Jess L. Goodman, Fort Benning; Mrs. Harold Smith, Fortson; and Mrs. Dick Sweeney, Phoenix, Ariz.; a daughter-in-law, Mrs. Leroy Ellis, Louisburg, N.C.; two sons, Dr. W. Y. Ellis, Newnan, and Ted Ellis, Pine Mountain; three sisters, Mrs. R. G. Ross, Miss Mae A. Ellis, and Miss Dora Ellis, all of Charlotte, N.C., and 17 grandchildren.

# Corn Meal Enriched in Pine Mountain

*The Columbus Enquirer*, July 13, 1959

An enrichment process added to Durand Miller's gristmill last week will put more "stick-to-the-ribs" ingredients in his typically southern corn meal.

With the assistance of John Noland, extension nutrition expert, Athens, and Forrest Salter, Harris County agricultural agent, Miller installed the gadget, which trickles out two ounces of vitamins, minerals and iron into each bushel of corn meal.

Enriched meal is sold across the counter in the local stores, but farmers bringing in corn by the bushel for grinding have missed out on the extra vitamins in their cornbread.

Each half pound of meal will contain 100 per cent of the minimum daily requirement of Vitamin B-1, and the following percentages of the minimum daily requirement of these other essential minerals: iron – 65, calcium – 33, riboflavin – 50, and niacin – 80.

Miller processes an average of 30 bushels per day with his small mill in Pine Mountain. The vitamins and minerals are supplied from the Extension Department on a nonprofit basis and is one phase of its nutrition program for the state.

# Retired Pine Mountain Police Chief Still Interested in Safety

*The Columbus Enquirer*, 1959

A. W. Johnson, retired chief of police for Pine Mountain, recently praised the new traffic code adopted for the city calling it as "a sign of progress."

Johnson served as city police chief for 21 years before his retirement in 1958. He served during this time not only as police chief but as superintendent of water works and sanitation department and was in charge of street maintenance.

Johnson began his service in Chipley on Jan. 1, 1937. He took particular interest in the children in the community and was very interested in safety measures for school children. He helped with the organization of the school patrol. Mr. and Mrs. Johnson lost their youngest son in an auto accident shortly after his graduation from high school and have been deeply interested in the safety of youth since this tragedy.

Earl Phillips, mayor of Pine Mountain, commended Johnson for his record during the term of service and said that he was not only a good officer but an outstanding citizen. His hobby of growing flowers around his own home and other spots in the city added much to the beautification of Pine Mountain. His hobby was shared with the sick and shut-ins, and many flowers from his garden were used in church, school and civic buildings for decoration on special occasions.

Mr. and Mrs. Johnson operated the City Café a few years ago in Pine Mountain. Their place of business was a meeting place for the young people after school and Mrs. Johnson was "Ma Johnson" to most of the students. Both Chief Johnson and Mrs. Johnson enjoyed working with young people and were always on hand for ball games and school activities. They are very proud of their two grandsons, Donnie and Robert Johnson, both football players for the University of Florida and Jacksonville High School, respectively.

Since his retirement, he and Mrs. Johnson have purchased a small farm at Big Springs community, a short distance from Pine Mountain. They plan to expand their hobbies with flowers and plants and recently added six beehives for additional enjoyment.

Johnson said that his 21 years of service to the people of Pine Mountain were very pleasant years. "The officials and citizens of the small city were my friends and were always very cooperative," he said.

# On a Troup County Dairy Farm ...
# They Found the Good Life

*The Columbus Ledger-Enquirer Sunday Magazine*,
February 21, 1960

Why does a young couple choose to live in the country on a dairy farm when so many of their friends are seeking an easier living in the city?

"Well, it has always been my ambition to operate my own dairy," said Eugene Scott, recently chosen Troup County's Outstanding Young Farmer of the Year.

"I like cows, I enjoy living in the country and I believe this is the best way for me to make a good substantial living," he continued.

"I enjoy living in the country too," chimed in Gene's attractive young wife, the former Miss Hazel Webb, "and there is plenty of room for children to play. We have good roads, all the modern conveniences and it's just a short distance to schools, churches, shopping and recreation areas."

Gene and Hazel, with their two-year-old daughter Lynne, live in a century-old farm house which they have completely remodeled on a dairy farm they purchased in October 1958. Located a short distance northwest of Pine Mountain, Ga., just across the county line in Troup, the farm was in a rundown condition until Gene began to build it up.

"The dairy barn is plenty large enough, it has 32 stanchions, but it hadn't been used for several years and needed quite a bit of repair," Gene told me.

"And one of the first things I did after buying the farm was to have the pasture soil tested," he added.

"I use four to six hundred pounds of fertilizer per acre and a ton of lime on some, as recommended by the results of the tests."

---

He has 40 acres in oats, rye grass, and rye, and 20 acres in crimson clover. The remaining acreage in the 240-acre farm is in permanent pasture (Bermuda grass).

"I plan to improve what I have instead of adding more land," he explained. "Quality will mean more than quantity, and I don't want land that I can't adequately take care of."

Gene has a herd of 40 dairy cows and is milking 34 of this number. He has 25 heifers which he is raising for replacements. Since the barn holds 32 cows at the time, he would like to build his herd up to 64 milkers. "Right now, however, I am more interested in production than in the number of cows," he says.

He believes three things are essential in reaching the maximum in production -- a good cow, good feeding and good management.

"I have used artificial breeding for about four years, and I believe this will be another factor in good milk production," he said. "I plan to increase this practice from 80 per cent to 100 per cent in my herd by next fall."

Most of Gene's cows are Holsteins, with a few Jerseys and several Guernseys. He raised most of his cattle and says this is more economical than buying grown animals.

"I KNOW the cow when I raise her," he said, "and then, too, there's less danger of bringing disease into the herd. I've never had a case of brucellosis," he explained. "I sure would hate to bring an infected cow into the dairy."

Gene's typical day begins at 5 a.m. He hasn't installed a pipeline milker so he and his Negro helper pour the milk from the electric-milker pails into the refrigerated holding tank. The 300-gallon stainless steel tank holds four milkings. Approximately 2,000 pounds of milk is picked up every other day by the tank truck from Wells Dairies Cooperative in Columbus.

"The tank is a great improvement over the 10-gallon cans stored in the old-type milk cooler," Gene pointed out. "And much easier to handle."

The cows are turned to pasture and the barn thoroughly cleaned before Gene goes up to the house for breakfast each morning in the attractive kitchen with the pine-paneled cabinets.

"The calves are fed, the fences checked and briars cleared from patches along with other jobs between breakfast and lunch time," he told me. "At other times of the year I may be sowing, preparing ground or putting out fertilizer.

"At 2 o'clock I put out the hay for the cows, at 3 I turn them in the oats and at 4 we bring them to the milking barn. We finish up around 6:30," he added, "and then I relax with my family."

Gene sings in the choir at the First Baptist Church in Pine Mountain and is president of the Pleasant Grove Community Club. The club recently won a blue ribbon in a countywide community improvement contest.

Hazel was a den mother for the Cub Scouts at South Highland Presbyterian Church near LaGrange for two years before they moved to Pine Mountain.

She helps with Vacation Bible School during the summer. Keeping up with venturesome little Lynne and running errands for Gene keep her busy.

"We had a very nice garden last spring," Hazel informed me. "I filled the freezer with vegetables, and when we used up part of those we killed a beef. We raised two pigs and put one of those in the freezer, too. Gene raised 25 fryers last year, and we have enough hens to supply us with all the eggs we need," she added.

"What about milk and butter?" I asked, as one dairyman's wife to another.

"I buy pasteurized milk for Lynne," she said. "We use some sweet milk from the dairy, but we buy all our buttermilk and butter. I haven't started churning yet."

Gene and Hazel met during a revival meeting at Pleasant Grove Methodist Church after Hazel's parents moved to the community from Moreland. Hazel finished high school at Newnan, went to Berry College at Rome for one year then transferred to LaGrange College to be near her parents.

Gene attended Rosemont High School where he was a member of the FFA Club and 4-H Club. He served as president of the FFA Club for two years. He built a dairy barn on his parents' farm in Pleasant Grove Community and started shipping milk shortly after graduating from Rosemont. There were 20 cows in his first milking herd.

The young couple married in June 1956 and continued dairying on Gene's parents' farm until they purchased the farm at Pine Mountain.

Hazel said she helped Gene with his milking machines and helped wash up after milkings until just before Lynne was born.

"We enjoy doing things together," they both said.

While showing me through the spacious rooms of their recently remodeled house, Hazel pointed to her new automatic washer.

"We got that with pecan money," she said. "We sold 7,600 pounds of pecans from the 89 trees on the place. It's nice to have an additional income during the winter."

How does Gene feel about being the Outstanding Young Farmer of the Year?

"I was surprised," he said. "They must have not had many names on that list and just chose one at random," he added modestly.

Records of those nominated were studied carefully by F. T. Evans, Troup County agriculture agent; Lee Barr, assistant agent; Henry Neal, vocational agriculture instructor at Troup High, and William Hudson, president of Troup Co. Farm Bureau. They all agreed that Gene is indeed an outstanding young farmer.

# City Plans to Take on New "Lighting"

*The Pine Mountain Review*, April 22, 1960

Detailed plans for an adequate street lighting program for the City of Pine Mountain will be presented to the city council at a called meeting this week.

The plans were drawn up by representatives of the Georgia Power Company and were presented to members of the street lighting committee, appointed during the recent Clean-Up campaign, by Melvin Hunt of Columbus.

The plans include several of the new type mercury florescent lights as well as installation of additional incandescent fixtures.

More than twenty new lampposts will be placed throughout the business area and at spots near churches and school areas, should the new plans be adopted by the council.

Members of the committee, which includes Mrs. Fletcher Chapman, Sr., Mrs. Ruth Bryant and Mrs. Earl Phillips, have passed out copies of the plans for study by council prior to the meeting scheduled for later this week. Mrs. Chapman, retiring president of the Chipley Woman's Club, stated that the new lighting system would be quite an improvement over the present lighting and would add much to the attractiveness of Pine Mountain.

# Colored News

*The Pine Mountain Review*, April 1960

by Mary G. Hixon

The Good Neighbor Health Club for Negroes was organized March 23 in a meeting with health officials in Hamilton. Assisting with the organization of the club were Mrs. Pearl Stanford, county health nurse, Dr. Mary Tiller, supervisor from Columbus, Mrs. Christian of Columbus and Walter M. Moore, county sanitarian. Harrison Miller, Negro county agent will serve as county chairman. Miss A. A. Copeland will preside over monthly meetings. Mrs. Hudson, secretary in Hamilton district, Rev. O. S. Copeland, Shiloh; Mrs. G. Hixon and B. W. McGee, Pine Mountain representatives. Each district will hold its own meetings each month.

Next county-wide meeting will be at Carver High School on May 4. All parents and committee members are urged to be present. Mrs. Stanford will speak on the subject, "Cleanliness."

Mr. and Mrs. Willie Shepherd, Mrs. Cameron, Mrs. Whatley visited Mrs. Emily Sturdivant in Atlanta Sunday. She is confined to her home with a broken hip.

Mr. and Mrs. Wayman Cameron and daughters, Irma Jean and Bonnie, of Atlanta, spent the weekend with his mother, Mrs. Ollie Bell Cameron, and brother, Howard.

Mrs. Essie Bryant and other relatives were called to Montgomery, Ala., last week due to the illness of an aunt, Mrs. Eva Whitable. Mrs. Bryant returned home Thursday, leaving Mrs. Whitable slightly improved.

Mrs. Dennie Fannins visited relatives in Atlanta recently.

Bethany Baptist Church urges all members and especially group captains to be present Sunday.

Contributions will go toward remodeling the interior of the church.

Beautiful shrubbery has been put out and is being put out around many homes in Pine Mountain. -- some around homes that have never had shrubbery before. As the old saying goes -- a woman's work is never done inside the home. I am sure the men will lend a helping hand on the outside.

*Note by Mrs. Champion, 2008: Mary George Hixson brought her news to me each week and I sent it along to The Pine Mountain Review. She died several years ago.*

# 15 Thousand Mob Kennedy at Little White House in Warm Springs

*The Pine Mountain Review*, October 14, 1960

### By John White

*(The Pine Mountain Review editor's note: John White, 16, a member of the Junior class of Harris County High School, presented his press card from the Pine Mountain Review to officials at Warm Springs Monday afternoon and, to the envy of his fellow schoolmates, got a ringside seat during the Kennedy speech. With press representatives from newspapers throughout the state seated around him, John took notes, shook hands with Senator Kennedy, and interviewed several of the dignitaries. The following is his account of the activities.)*

Democratic presidential Nominee Sen. John F. Kennedy made his first major address in Georgia here Monday to a cheering, screaming, and applauding crowd between 13,444 to 15,000.

With the words "he's here" pandemonium broke loose. Spectators (some of whom had spent Sunday night in automobiles) crushed in -- insistently thrusting their hands at the Massachusetts Senator.

To add to the confusion, two High School bands were playing "Good Times are Here Again," the Democratic theme song, along with Graham Jackson, personal musician of FDR. Down front in the area reserved for newsmen and photographers, state troopers twice had to clear the great press of spectators that had filtered through the police lines.

Draped above and slightly to the rear of Senator Kennedy as he spoke from the front of the Little White

*Photograph courtesy of John White*

**John White (left) being presented with the AP Radio-Television award by Lamar Matthews, Broadcast Editor of The Associated Press Atlanta Bureau, in 1964**

House, was a tattered presidential Naval flag that flew from the masts of U. S. ships which carried FDR to many of his historical meetings abroad.

Sitting on the front porch were such dignitaries as Gov. Vandiver, Senator Herman Talmadge, James Gray, Chairman of the Ga. Democratic Party, U. S. representatives Phil Landrum, J. L. Pilcher, John Flint, and E. L. Forrester, former Govs. Ellis Arnall, M. E. Thompson and E. D. Rivers, George Smathers of Florida. (Incidentally, it was noted by this reporter that Sen. Talmadge, when introduced, received more applause than did Sen. Kennedy.)

Although Kennedy's speech was a good, crowd pleasing one, nothing was said of his plans for action if elected. The main theme was of medicare and problems.

"Two million handicapped or disabled people in America today could be rehabilitated if the funds and services were available," he said, "but instead we are providing for 88,000." "We can do better," he continued, "must do better -- if we are to live up to the 'spirit of Warm Springs.'"

"In meeting the problems of the '60's, our responsibilities are many. Our critics will be strong. But I ask you to remember that here at Warm Springs they found among Franklin D. Roosevelt's papers a speech that he had written, but never delivered, and it closed with these words: 'The only limit to our realization of tomorrow will be our doubts of today. Let us move forward with a strong and active faith.'"

After the address, this reporter exclusively interviewed James Gray and Sen. George Smathers. Gray, more enthusiastic about the Democratic vote in the "solid south" said, "I expect a larger Democratic majority in Georgia than ever before, even in the years '52 and '56." Smathers, a little less optimistic, commented, "Maybe not all southern states will go solidly."

Letter to News Editor

Dear Mrs. Champion,

I am writing you in regard to an article concerning Senator John Kennedy's recent visit to Warm Springs. Having covered the arrival of our next President here in Columbus and following him on to Warm Springs for additional radio coverage there, I am most pleased that the REVIEW was able to give its readers who could not be there a near perfect report of what went on.

What impressed me even more, however, was the fact that your front page account was written by a sixteen year old boy, John White, from Harris County High. After reading the account several times, I came to the conclusion that one newsman should congratulate another for any job well done. For a boy of sixteen, I feel that John showed a deep insight about what the public wants in a news-feature story, and how it should be given in accurate and understandable form. Having had experience in both radio and newspaper reporting, and having been immersed in the melee, as John must have been before reaching his vantage point, I know he did a fine job.

Thank you for sending us THE PINE MOUNTAIN REVIEW. Big Johnny Reb is always interested in its Georgia neighbors.

Yours truly,
Bill Cullen
News Director
WDAK, Columbus

*Note by Mrs. Champion, 2008: John B. White, Jr. wrote a weekly school news column and, with a press card from THE PINE MOUNTAIN REVIEW, he went to Warm Springs to cover John Kennedy's campaign speech for me. In the next issue of LIFE magazine there was a large photograph of 16-year-old John in the press box, center front, with the media "big boys." Later, he was news director at radio station WTRP while a student at LaGrange College.*

*John retired from The Coca-Cola Company in June 2000, after 34 years of service. At the time of his retirement he was assistant vice president, Governmental Relations, a position he had held since 1993. Along with being a consultant to the company, he is secretary to the Management Development Committee of the company's Board of Directors. From 1981 to 1993, he served as executive assistant to the president of the company. He previously served as manager of Media Relations and Industry and Community Affairs.*

*Before joining The Coca-Cola Company, he was an editor for United Publishing Company and served as press secretary to Republican gubernatorial candidate Howard H. (Bo) Callaway.*

*He serves on the Board of the Atlanta Symphony Orchestra and is chair of the Board's Strategic Planning and Public Affairs committees. He also serves on the board of Atlanta Public Broadcasting and on the Board of Visitors, Terry Sanford Institute of Public Policy, Duke University.*

# Pine Mountain Industry

## Pine Mountain Expects New Tenant Shortly for Plant
*The Columbus Enquirer*, November 4, 1960

New tenant for the Pine Mountain manufacturing building, formerly occupied by Dacula Sportswear Inc. is expected to be announced within the next two weeks, Mayor Earl Phillips said Thursday.

Mayor Phillips, who also is president of the Chipley Development Corp., owners of the building, said that three manufacturing companies met with the corporation developers Tuesday afternoon and into the night.

Representatives of a New York company flew by jet to Atlanta Tuesday afternoon and arrived in Pine Mountain early in the evening. In addition to the conferences with the other two companies, both Georgia concerns, contacts have been made from several other manufacturers.

Phillips said that every effort is being made to reach a decision and have a plant in operation in the building formerly occupied by the Dacula Sportswear Corp. before the some 80 employees get scattered or find employment in other areas.

Goods and equipment are being moved from the Dacula plant and will be sold at public outcry here on Monday at 10 a.m. to satisfy labor liens of former employees who filed for more than two weeks back pay.

The plant was closed abruptly on Oct. 19 following a communique from Howard R. Hale, Sr. of Atlanta, president of the corporation, which revealed that he "was running away from too much pressure" and would not be back to continue operation of the company. Hale's whereabouts remain unknown.

In addition to the Pine Mountain plant, the Dacula Corporation also had factories in Duluth and Dacula, Ga., before the latter plant was destroyed by fire last spring.

Industry in Pine Mountain began in 1947 when the citizens organized the Chipley Development Corp. A total of 53 stockholders put up $60,400 to erect a building which was leased by a Columbus clothing manufacturer. For a period of 10 years Schwobilt suits for men were manufactured here until the death of Simon Schwob resulted in termination of the Pine Mountain plant.

In seeking a new industry to occupy the modern, functional structure, individual citizens purchased 25 per cent of the stock of Dacula Sportswear, Inc. A total of 12 to 15 thousand jackets were produced each week from July 1957 until shortly before the plant closed in October. Plans had been drawn up for doubling floor space of the main building but were postponed until plant operations could be increased with a more optimistic outlook.

"We lost our stock in the company," one stockholder commented, "but having about 80 persons on the payroll for a period of almost three years meant a lot to the town. We don't intend to look back, but forward."

Mayor Phillips, who succeeded the late J. O. Kimbrough as president of the Chipley Development Corp., serves on the corporation's board of directors along with A. H. Anderson, vice president; W. Ken Askew, secretary; B. W. Dismukes, treasurer, and the following members: Durand Miller, Vance Smith and Fletcher Chapman.

## New Firm Will Open Pine Mountain Plant
*The Columbus Enquirer*, December 21, 1960

Chipley Outerwear, Inc., a new corporation, has purchased the abandoned equipment of Dacula Sportswear Inc. and will open a new plant here in February.

The Chipley Outerwear group bid $8,050 for machinery and other equipment of Dacula, which was put up for sale by the federal government.

Ken Askew, Pine Mountain attorney, said the new group will begin operation of the plant around Feb. 1 with about 35 employees.

Askew said that Jack Smith, who was formerly with the Dacula plant, will manage the new undertaking which will manufacture about the same clothing as did the other company.

The opening of the new company also may lead to expansion of the local operation and the establishment of a "shipping point" in Pine Mountain, Askew said.

Askew said that the building in which the new plant will operate is still locally owned and that the new firm will have about the same contract as was held by the Dacula group before the firm's president abandoned the plant.

# Many Signs Offer 'Bargains' for Pine Mountain

*The Columbus Enquirer*, November 3, 1960

Halloween pranks that have become a tradition in Pine Mountain were carried out again this year.

"Fire Sale" signs were found on front doors of business establishments, advertising automobiles for ten cents, and merchandise at ridiculous prices.

The auto belonging to Ken Askew, city attorney, bore a placard offering it for quick sale at one dollar. An old farm wagon in front of an auto sales shop contained a message that any person with an automobile could possible get up a trade for the wagon.

A Nixon-Lodge banner mysteriously appeared across the main highway leading into town from the South.

A few windows were soaped, getting merchants out early Tuesday morning washing and scrubbing doors and windows, but on a whole, the ghosts and goblins were out for pranks and not destruction.

# She Has Lived for a Century

*The Columbus Enquirer*, January 22, 1961

Mrs. Elizabeth Williams Anderson of Pine Mountain, Ga., is one of the few persons living who can say, "I remember Sherman's march through Georgia."

A hundred years old last Wednesday, Jan. 18, Mrs. Anderson lived through the entire Civil War in this section of the state.

Although she was only four years old when the Yankee soldiers came, she remembers the strange-clad men removing handmade bricks from the walk in front of her Georgia farm home. She also recalls how the Northerners threw the bricks about the yard, creating a wild disorder.

Mrs. Anderson, one of 12 children of Asa and Nancy Herring Williams, was born in 1861 in Muscogee County near Fortson. When she was a very small child her family moved to Meriwether County and since that time she has spent most of her life in Meriwether and Harris Counties.

All of her brothers and sisters have died, and she is the sole survivor of the family.

"I married when I was 23," Mrs. Anderson says. "In Harris County," she adds. Tom Anderson, her husband, was known as the tallest man in the county, according to some of the elder citizens of Pine Mountain. His six feet seven inches towered over everyone in the area.

"Anyone over six feet tall didn't have to pay poll tax," one of the senior citizens recalls. "And Tom Anderson sure qualified for exemption."

Mr. and Mrs. Anderson celebrated their 63rd wedding anniversary before his death 16 years ago.

Today Mrs. Anderson makes her home with a daughter, Mrs. Robert Myhand, at King's Gap, just east of the city of Pine Mountain. A son, Joe C. Anderson, lives at Midland, Ga. There are five generations in Mrs.

Anderson's family now, including her two children, five grandchildren, 15 great-grandchildren and 11 great-great-grandchildren. Most of these descendants reside in Muscogee and Harris counties.

Believed to be Harris County's oldest living white citizen, Mrs. Anderson is still very active. She believes in arising early and is usually awake by 4 a.m., up by daylight and ready for breakfast at 7 o'clock. She frequently teases her daughter about sleeping late.

When the weather is suitable, Mrs. Anderson rides into town with Mrs. Myhand and likes to sit in the car and watch people pass while Mrs. Myhand shops.

She enjoys spending the day with friends in the area and, before Christmas, visited for several days with her son's family in Midland.

"I crocheted until I was 95," Mrs. Anderson explains. Failing eyesight has limited her sewing activities, however, and her greatest pleasure at present is chatting with visitors, both relatives and friends, who drop in to see her.

"The family has been awfully good about coming to see mama," Mrs. Myhand said. "Some of the grandchildren are here nearly every weekend."

Mrs. Myhand's son and his wife recently became the parents of a little girl, and Mrs. Anderson could hardly wait for them to come over "so I can hold the baby."

A member of the Primitive Baptist Church near Durand, Mrs. Anderson enjoys preaching services and revival meetings. The last service she attended was in November of last year, but she plans to go again when the weather is a little warmer.

On Sunday mornings she sits in her living room and listens to sermons from the Columbus TV stations. Television and radio give her many hours of pleasure, according to Mrs. Myhand. Her favorite programs are religious or church programs, and music, any type music, even a little jazz now and then.

Cornbread, buttermilk and turnip greens are still her favorite foods, but she enjoys modern dishes along with the old. Unless the weather is extremely cold, Mrs. Anderson eats at the table with her daughter. On cold days, Mrs. Myhand takes a tray to her room.

Mrs. Anderson has lived through a century in which the greatest changes in the history of the nation have taken place. Now the headlines again paint a troubled picture, and it makes us wonder what the next century will bring. Perhaps Mrs. Anderson's philosophy of simple living and love for one's fellow man is a good example for us all.

# Fire Brought to Fireman by Rail

*The Pine Mountain Review*, February 16, 1961

Members of the Pine Mountain Volunteer Fire Department had the fire truck waiting Monday evening when a fire was brought into town by rail.

Bill Bradford, engineer on the Man O' War, notified station master W. C. McLaney when he discovered smoke coming from the refrigeration car as the train reached Tip Top at 4:30.

Hacking their way through the outer wall, local firemen sprayed water into the insulation between the inner and outer walls of the unit which was loaded with cut flowers bound for the Midwest.

When smoke continued to pour out from the interior of the car, the unit was uncoupled from the train and moved to the track near the loading platform of the depot. Approximately 30 or 40 boxes of gladioli and other flowers were unloaded in order to property extinguish the blaze.

The flowers were reloaded on an express car before the train continued on to Atlanta after being held up for about an hour.

# Troup Barn Discloses Coffin Box
# Made in 1849

*The Columbus Enquirer*, March 30, 1961

"Curiosity seekers have offered me as much as a hundred dollars for that old box stored in the loft of my barn, but I aim to keep it right where it is," Byron Butts, 78, Route 2, Pine Mountain said.

The "box" is an old coffin box, shaped like an oversized mummy case, and has been on the farm since 1849, Butts said.

According to a story told by Butts' father, William Butts (who lost a leg in the Confederate Army, and was tax receiver of Troup County at the time of his death before 1900) the box was used to bring home the body of Paschal P. Sturdivant.

Sturdivant had gone to Mississippi in 1849 to see the daughter of a family that had migrated to the West from southern Troup County.

The young man became ill and died during his visit. His family was notified that his body had been interred in Mississippi.

The parents decided that they wanted Paschal buried at home so the grieving father set out by wagon to bring the body back to Georgia.

"My father told me that Joel Sturdivant had the oversized box made so he could pack charcoal around the smaller wooden coffin which held the body," Butts said.

"Paschal was the first person to be buried in the Sturdivant Cemetery, a short distance from the house where the family lived," he added.

Butts now resides in the old Sturdivant house today. The box was in the barn when he bought the place a number of years ago.

---

"It holds a good bit of corn – for the cows and mules," he chuckled. A visit to the barn loft found the coffin box intact, with about half a bushel corn inside.

Butts quickly pointed out Paschal Sturdivant's grave among the rows in the old cemetery. Engraved on the heavy marker, which was broken and propped up at the the head of the grave, is the following: *Paschal P. Sturdivant, son of Melinda & Joel Sturdivant, born Aug. 25th, 1825; died Aug. 16th, 1849. Aged 23 yrs. 11 months and 21 days.*

# Pine Mountain Reports
# Progress for Past Year

*The Columbus Enquirer*, January 13, 1962

The year 1961 left a lot of memories, mostly good ones, for the citizens of Pine Mountain.

Checking back over the news stories for 1961, we found that, as a whole, most events will be remembered pleasantly.

Of course there were deaths, fires, accidents and other tragic incidents, which marred the year for some of the families. On the other hand, there were the joys of births, weddings and outstanding social, civic and church events.

The year 1961 began on a bright note with the announcement of plans to open a new industry, Chipley Outerwear, Inc., in the early spring. For more than 60 persons, this meant an opportunity to work here at home, instead of having to seek employment elsewhere.

The local Chamber of Commerce got off to a good start last January under the leadership of Gilbert Wildes; Bryan Patrick, successfully underwent a most serious operation in a New York hospital, and Mrs. Elizabeth Anderson observed her 100th birthday on Jan. 18.

The ice storm almost paralyzed the town the last few days of January, but in spite of the inconveniences of no phones, no heat and no water, there were some pretty hilarious things to remember. (What about that canned chicken that hit the ceiling when the fire on the hearth finally got hot?)

The new post office officially opened Feb. 1, adding to the attractiveness of the town and to the convenience of handling the increased volume of mail.

The Heart Fund Drive in Pine Mountain exceeded the goal of $200 by $125. Mrs. O. D. Marshall was named head of the Harris County Education Association, and discussions began around town regarding the sale of a portion of the Roosevelt State Park to the Ida Cason Callaway Foundation.

It rained the first day of March and it rained the next day, and the next, and for many more days. On the roads coming in to Pine Mountain, bridges were washed away and Mr. and Mrs. C. W. Lee of Salem community were injured when their car struck a washout.

National 4-H week was observed and research on Civil War history in this area began throughout the county.

Dr. Guy Adkinson, president of Norman College, Norman Park, Ga., was guest speaker at the annual sunrise service at the Gardens, the eight graders at Chipley School went on their annual class trip to Chattanooga and, during the latter part of April, Alvin S. Davis, of LaGrange, was appointed vice president of the Ida Cason Callaway Foundation.

Also in April, a compulsory dog inoculation program was established by the Health Department, under the direction of Walter Moore; John White won the State Literary Meet Declamation (Class B) Contest, and our neighbor, Cason J. Callaway, Sr., died at his Blue Springs home.

On April 28, the Chipley Woman's Club held a centennial celebration, with a display of relics and an old fashioned square dance.

The town voted May 17 for the school bonds which made it possible to begin on an addition to the local school. (The addition now is under construction.)

The Harris County FFA quartet won the statewide contest, Ellen Askew was awarded an honor scholarship to Mercer, Betty Champion won the Lion's Club math and science award, and Marjorie Champion was presented a medal from the Ga. Historical Commission for her essay on "Georgia at War – 1861."

Karl Bochsbichler of Austria came to live with Mr. and Mrs. Hopson Morgan on their dairy farm near Pine Mountain during the month of June. An exchange student, Karl was very impressed with local farming methods.

A site was selected during June for the construction of a new depot (now almost completed), and plans were made for straightening U. S. Highway 27 through the center of town. These plans are to be completed as soon as the old depot building is removed.

Mary Frances White received her degree in Home Economics from GSCW and was appointed home demonstration agent in Cobb County. An outstanding 4-H'er, Mary Frances attended her first 4-H camp in a bassinet at the age of three months.

In July, the Rev. Charles Clarke was appointed minister of the Chipley Methodist Church, the home demonstration club members aided patients at the State Hospital by making caddy bags, and on the 23rd, the new post office was dedicated in a formal ceremony. Mrs. Anderson, our 100-year-old citizen, died at her home July 9.

A Youth Revival was conducted by the Methodist Church in July, with a special service held at Dowdell's Knob atop Pine Mountain. The Durham family has a large attendance at its annual reunion, and Mr. and Mrs. Forest Champion, Sr. observed their 50th wedding anniversary by attending revival services at Bethany where they joined the church together a few days following their wedding.

School began the last week in August and, later, the college students left home. William Kimbrough served as president of the Harris Athletic Improvement Association which concentrated on building bleachers and steps at the Harris County football field.

On Oct. 6, Margot van Lennep of Wassenaar, Holland, became the bride of Don Taylor, in a ceremony at the local Methodist Church. This spring, Mrs. Taylor's tulips will lend a little Dutch flavor to our Southern hospitality.

An outstanding event of fall was the Fifth District PTA conference, held at the Methodist Church here Wed. Oct 11. The guest speaker was Mrs. Cicero Johnston, president of the state organization, who began her teaching career here at the Chipley School, as the former Miss Helen Landis.

In November, the Cub Pack was re-chartered at the Methodist Church and Mrs. Roxie Crossman, who resides with Mrs. Tom Hadley, observed her 100th birthday.

More than 50 days without rain created a drought in the area and local dairymen began digging into winter reserve of feed in order to keep up milk production.

Remodeling began on the 133-year-old Bethany Church, believed to be the first church constituted in Harris County. A steeple, choir loft, and stained-glass windows were added and the interior redecorated.

An East Point resident lost his life in an accident here on Thanksgiving Day when he lost control of his car and crashed into Tom Livingston's service station.

In December, the Chipley Development Corp. declared a 3 per cent dividend on earnings for 1961, and reelected the entire slate of officers, with Mayor Earl J. Phillips, as president.

The year ended with a watch night service at the Baptist Church, and a special prayer for the new year was given as the old year bowed out.

# B. W. Dismukes, Jr.,
# Volunteer Fire Chief

*The Columbus Enquirer*, February 7, 1962

B. W. Dismukes, Jr., is chief of the Volunteer Fire Department in Pine Mountain. He also owns and operates a plumbing and electric service company, serves as treasurer of the Chipley Development Corporation, is a city tax assessor, and takes a keen interest in projects undertaken by community, schools and churches – but when the fire alarm sounds, he drops everything and heads for the fire station.

He was instrumental in securing for the town a good used pumper and other firefighting equipment, by workers in a citywide canvass of property owners for funds. The drive was repeated two years ago in order to replace the truck with a later model.

His first experience as a volunteer fireman came while he was residing in a small town in Alabama about 30 years ago. When fire broke out in a residence on the corner of the street where he lived, Dismukes quickly rounded up the neighbors and put them to work watering down the adjourning houses with garden hose and bucket brigades.

Too late to save the first house, he knocked out windows and managed to save most of the family's furnishings before the roof began to fall in.

Dismukes is a native of Harris County, the son of the late B. W. and Emma Moody Dismukes. He was born March 26, 1903, on the family plantation near Dowdell's Knob at the foot of Pine Mountain. He attended Chipley elementary and Valley Plains High School in Harris County and later, while working in Missouri, studied engineering at Chicago Technical College.

Once, while returning to Georgia from Missouri, on a cold January day, Dismukes demonstrated his quick thinking in an emergency by plunging into an icy river to rescue a 12-year-old girl who was pinned in the wreckage of an overturned truck.

Dismukes worked with Allied engineers, and other companies, building dams on rivers in Georgia, Alabama, and Missouri, before returning to Harris County in 1935 with the National Park Service to assist in the development of Roosevelt State Park. The old Dismukes plantation site was a portion of the land he helped to develop.

Following his work with the Park Service, he supervised development of roads and other projects in an area embracing several counties. He received an appointment from Washington, through the C.A.A., as engineer for the construction of an airport at LaGrange, now the Callaway Airport.

He established his plumbing and electric business in Pine Mountain 14 years ago and took his son, Leroy, as his partner. As the business expanded, they erected a new, modern building on Center Street.

B. W. and Mrs. Dismukes, the former Irma Phillips of Warm Springs, also have a daughter, Lillian, who in addition to being her father's secretary and the wife of a Troup County dairyman (Hubert Champion), is an *Enquirer* state correspondent.

The volunteer fire chief's hobby is flying, and on sunny afternoons, between fire calls and business engagements, he hops into a little plane at the nearby Callaway Gardens Airport and takes off for a quick trip around the countryside. His three teen-aged grandchildren share his enthusiasm for flying.

# Zachry Death Shocks Citizens

*The Pine Mountain Review*, February 8, 1962

The unexpected death of Henry Zachry on Friday morning, Feb. 2, came as a shock to citizens of Pine Mountain and surrounding communities.

Mr. Zachry, 72, was president of the Farmers and Merchants Bank of Pine Mountain for 35 years and was busy during the first part of last week completing plans for the construction of a new bank building on the site of the old livery stable. He was at the bank most of the day on Thursday before his death on Friday morning at 10:15, following a heart attack at his home on King Avenue.

Funeral was held at 3 p.m. Sunday at First Baptist Church in Pine Mountain, with the Rev. Milton Rexrode, pastor, assisted by the Rev. Alec Copeland of Hamilton, conducting the service.

Pallbearers were W. H. Kimbrough, Ken Askew, Sam Whatley, Tom Livingston, Sr., Fletcher Chapman, Sr., and Vance Smith.

Honorary pallbearers were Roy Askew, H. C. Kimbrough, Jr., Dr. W. P. Ellis, Jesse McGee, Ruben Anderson, Maynard Dunn, Dayton Calhoun, Sr., George Teel, Durand Sivell and B. W. Williams.

Burial was in the Pine Mountain Cemetery, with Maddox Funeral Home in charge.

Mr. Zachry was the son of the late Lewis Hudson and Rebecca Ann Marsh Zachry. He was born July 23, 1889, at Smith's Cross Road (now southern edge of Salem Community), Harris County, where he held extensive farming interests until the time of his death.

A friend to all who knew him, Mr. Zachry was keenly interested in community development and in projects of improvement in civic, church and school areas.

He extended a helping hand both to organizations and individuals throughout the county.

Survivors include his wife, the former Clyde Spence; a daughter, Miss Bertha Ann Zachry; two sisters, Miss Pauline Zachry and Miss Zelma Zachry, all of Pine Mountain, a niece, Mrs. Max O'Neal, Eastman, Ga., and two nephews, Ronald and Alf Mullins, both of Pine Mountain.

# 'Home Town' Booster –
# Pine Mountain is Best for Askew

*The Columbus Enquirer*, February 20, 1962

Ken Askew is one of Pine Mountain's most enthusiastic "Better Home Town" boosters.

When Ken finished high school in 1940, the trend was, as it is today, for the youth of small communities to seek employment in the larger cities instead of settling down in the old hometown. Ken, however, was one of the few young people who wanted to seek a livelihood in a familiar environment.

His studies at Mercer University were interrupted by World War II. After three years in the infantry, he returned to Mercer and graduated with an A.B. degree in August 1947.

Pine Mountain was without a practicing attorney, so Ken decided to make this his goal. He returned to Mercer and received his L.L.B. in June 1950.

After he set up his law office, he pitched in with local leaders to make the hometown a better town in many respects. He was one of the driving forces behind a campaign which boosted Chipley (now Pine Mountain) to a first-place award in the Georgia Power "Better Home Town" contest a few years ago.

He also spent long hours taking "before" and "after" photos of improvement projects, and compiling a scrapbook that told the story of accomplishments.

Today, Ken, 38, is not only a successful lawyer in his home town, he is a partner in his father's insurance agency, one of the directors of the local bank, a deacon and Sunday School teacher at First Baptist Church, a member of the church choir, and a member of the local school board.

*Photograph courtesy of Ken Askew*

**W. Ken Askew**
**Photo made while he was a**
**student in law school at Mercer**
**University.**

He is past Master of Chipley Masonic Lodge, and past president of the Pine Mountain Chamber of Commerce, and is presently serving as attorney for the Chipley Development Corporation, a local industry-boosting company.

If he had the time, sports would be his hobby, he says. He enjoys an occasional game of golf, swimming in the summer, and attending basketball games.

Ken is the son of Ruth Kendrick Askew and Roy Askew, who have been associated with the local bank for more than 50 years.

The young lawyer is married to the former Marguerite Foster, who came to Chipley with her dentist father while she was a high school student. The Askew's daughter, Ruth Ellen, 18, is a freshman at Mercer. They also have a son, Jeff, age 3 years.

Ken says that the youth of today will find more opportunities in the old hometown – they will have to be discovered by some – but well worth looking for.

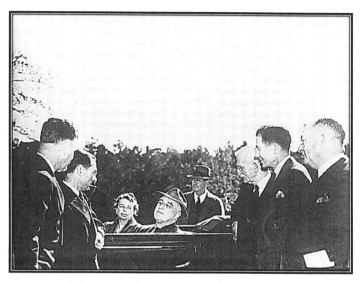

*Photograph courtesy of Chad Kimbrough*

This photograph of President Franklin Roosevelt was taken on Friday, November 24, 1939, at Warm Springs, Georgia, following the dedication of the new Warm Springs community house named in honor of his mother, Mrs. Sarah Delano Roosevelt.

Left to right: Tap Bennett, manager of the Pine Mountain Valley resettlement project; W. L. Miller, State Highway Board chairman; Mrs. Roosevelt, President Roosevelt; unnamed Secret Service agent; Henry C. Kimbrough of Chipley; James L. Gillis, Highway Board member; and Clem E. Wright, assistant chief engineer of the Highway Department.

# Plans for New Bank on Old Stable Site

*The Columbus Enquirer*, February 1962

*The Columbus Enquirer's editor's note: Some of the facts for this article were given to Mrs. Champion by Henry Zachry on Tuesday afternoon before his death the following Friday morning.*

The old livery stable on McDougald Avenue is being torn down. The site is to be cleared for the construction of a new building to house the local Farmers and Merchants Bank, a spokesman for the bank directors stated this week.

With the removal of the old stable and another old building standing next to it, Pine Mountain will have erased all traces of the horse and buggy days. The old blacksmith shop, which stood on the corner of the same street, was torn down to make room for the new post office, completed last February. The wisteria-covered fount where horses were hitched and watered in the center of town is gone and the spot is now a paved parking area for automobiles.

The old livery stable's demise has stirred up the memories of some of the town's senior citizens.

No one is quite sure when the old building was erected, but according to Henry Griggs it was prior to 1905.

Harold (Mr. Tobe) Magruder, 89, one of Pine Mountain's most active senior citizens, recalls some of the events that took place around the old stable in the year 1906.

"That was the year we had eight killings in Chipley," Mr. Tobe stated. "We even got credit for some that took place up the road near LaGrange."

According to a few others, who also resided here during that time, the "wild west" reputation of the town was such that passengers were warned to "lie down on the floor of the train when you pass through Chipley -- lest you be struck by flying bullets."

The old livery stable was the scene of the climax of one quarrel which ended in two deaths. The argument over a debt for moonshine whiskey waxed hot while Hoke Smith, candidate for governor of Georgia, was making a campaign speech in the adjourning grove next to the Baptist Church, according to present-day residents who were on hand for the barbeque and speechmaking that day in 1906. When the killer ran through the old stable, the crowd turned away from the speaker and became a posse.

Things begin to simmer down after a few years and the old livery stable became a meeting place for checker games and exchange of some tall horse-swapping tales.

Olin Durham's vet office was close by and Dr. Glass' drug store, on the same street, stocked the usual liniment, good for both man and horse.

George Nelson "taxied" drummers to and from nearby communities in the stable's best buggy, and mules were for hire to anyone preparing gardens for planting.

The stable changed hands now and then during the early years of its existence, some of the first operators were Bob Middlebrooks, Oscar Tucker and Ben Fletcher. The Chipley Livestock Co., ran the stable for a short time and Charlie M. Kimbrough took over in 1913. Henry C. Kimbrough became the owner following Mr. Charlie's death and the stable was operated by various local citizens, including Henry Zachry and H. C. Kimbrough, Jr.

One day in 1932, a resident of Warm Springs came over to Chipley and mentioned to Henry Kimbrough, Sr., that he needed a mule to pull the trash wagon on his place.

"I'll send one over for you," Mr. Kimbrough said. "No, I would like to see what you have," the buyer replied.

According to the story related by Mr. Kimbrough's relatives, the two went over to the stable where Mr.

Kimbrough with an eye for future business, quoted a reduced price on the mule.

The buyer knew that he was getting a bargain, so he snapped up the offer.

The mule buyer was Franklin D. Roosevelt, then governor of New York. The next year, after he became president, he often told how he "made forty dollars off Henry Kimbrough down in Chipley, Ga., on a mule trade."

Mule trading began to slow down with the appearance of tractors and trucks on the farms, and a few years ago the old stable was closed.

The new bank building will be the fourth construction to recently replace buildings from the early days of the town. The post office, school house and depot have added to the long-range city beautification program under way in creating a more attractive town for local residents and tourists.

# Askew Elected Bank Prexy

*The Pine Mountain Review*, March 1, 1962

Roy Askew was this week elected president of the Farmers and Merchants bank at Pine Mountain. He succeeds the late Henry Zachry who held the position for 35 years prior to his death on Feb. 9, this year.

Miss Bertha Ann Zachry was elected to the board of directors in her father's place. Other members of the board include Ken Askew, W. H. Kimbrough and P. H. Layfield.

Polly (Mrs. Leroy) Dismukes was recently made assistant cashier and Louise (Mrs. Joe) Hamlin was employed this month as a teller.

Other members of the bank personnel are: Louis Askew, assistant cashier; Eula Mae (Mrs. Andrew) Sivell and Martha (Mrs. John) Wharton, bookkeepers, and Dester (Mrs. William) Neal, secretary to cashier. Neut Askew is a part-time employee.

The newly elected president will also serve as cashier, a spokesman for the board of directors stated.

Mr. Askew is a native of Harris County, the son of the late Albert Wallace and Fanny Davis Askew, members of pioneer families of this area. He attended school at Hopewell and Chipley, and studied at the University of Georgia. He taught school at Chipley for a short while before beginning his career in banking more than 50 years ago.

His first assignment was cashier of a Durand, Ga., branch of Farmers and Merchants. The branch was closed in 1912 after operating less than a year.

Mr. Askew's months at Durand was time well spent for it was there he met a young music teacher at the local school. She was Ruth Kendrick from Plains. They were married that year and will celebrate their 50th wedding anniversary this April.

Mr. Askew returned to Chipley and worked at the bank continuously until the present, except for a brief period in the early 1920s when he operated an auto sales agency here.

An active member of the Pine Mountain Baptist Church, the bank president serves on the Board of Deacons and is a former Sunday School Superintendent. He is very active in church, community, school and civic affairs.

The Askews are the parents of four children, Roy Askew, Jr., deceased, Wallace Kendrick Askew, Pine Mountain attorney, Ida (Mrs. Leon) Blythe, of Columbus, and Alice, wife of a Cape Canaveral scientist, W. Meriwether Furlough. There are nine grandchildren and one great-grandchild.

Mr. Askew commented that the bank reflects the financial condition of the community. He modestly refused to go into details or to take any of the credit for the progress of the business. The only figures he made available revealed that in 1932 the total assets were approximately $75,000. Today, according to the latest report released, the assets are 3 million dollars.

Plans for construction of a new bank building on the site of the old livery stable will be continued, Mr. Askew said. He said that the plans drawn up by the late Mr. Zachry will be carried out in the not too distant future.

*Note by Mrs. Champion, 2008: The bank was not built on the site of the old livery stable. It was established in the area of Alf Mullins' grocery store, using the outer walls of the old store in the new building.*

---

# Pine Mountain Site of Many Changes

*The Pine Mountain Review*, March 1, 1962

The old middle-of-the-road depot in Pine Mountain is only a memory today.

The structure has been torn down and the site has been cleared. Work on straightening U. S. Highway 27 through the town is expected to begin within the next few weeks, according to Earl J. Phillips, mayor. The highway has already been surveyed by the State Highway Department.

Other changes are also taking place in Pine Mountain. The old livery stable on McDougald Ave. has been completely demolished and the site is being cleared for construction of a new building to house the Farmers and Merchants Bank.

Henry A. Mullins is retiring as a merchant and is selling out the stock in his general store on the corner of Center Street.

Mr. and Mrs. Jim Edgar, who recently moved to Pine Mountain from California, have purchased the former Patrick's Grocery and plan to open a dry goods and ready to wear business in the very near future. Mrs. Edgar is the daughter of Mr. and Mrs. Earl J. Phillips of Pine Mountain.

# Davis Retires as Carrier in
# Pine Mountain

*The Columbus Enquirer*, March 12, 1962

James Pope Davis, Sr. has retired from his rural mail route after 42 years of service.

Davis, who will be 65 on April 1, has been on sick leave for several months and was officially retired on Feb. 25, 42 years and one day from the day he began his career as a rural carrier.

His work began in 1920, on a rainy Tuesday. The previous Sunday was George Washington's birthday, so Monday was a holiday for postal employees. There was three days mail to deliver on his first trip, made in a model T over 30 miles of unpaved roads east of Chipley (now Pine Mountain).

That first day, according to Davis, was rather long. He arrived back in town about 4 p.m.

At the time Davis began his career, Chipley had five rural routes. In addition to Mr. Davis, the carriers were Sam Durham, Cooper Jenkins, Bill Lewis Jenkins and Hiram Jenkins. Mr. Davis is the only one of the group still living.

Through the years the roads were improved and the mail volume increased. Transportation facilities were also improved.

The five routes were consolidated into three, with Sam Durham, Hiram Jenkins and Mr. Davis as carriers. Durham and Jenkins both died several years ago after devoting more than 30 years each to the postal service.

Henderson Hopkins and Ernest Truitt, Jr. were appointed in their places. No appointment has been made for Davis' route as yet.

R. H. Dunlap was postmaster in Chipley in 1920 when Davis sorted out the mail for his first delivery run. In

February of last year, Davis helped Hubert Hadley, present Postmaster, and other local postal employees, move into the new modern post office on McDougald Ave.

"There have been a lot of changes in the last 42 years," Davis commented. "But better transportation and the new postal building have been among the greatest improvements in handling the increased mail volume here."

Davis was born in Harris County, near King's Gap, on April 1, 1897. He is the son of the late Madison and Clara Whitehead Davis.

He was married in 1922 to Miss Maree Cecil Cook, of Cochran, Ga., who died in 1954. They were parents of four children: James Pope Davis, Jr., of Greer, S. C.; Cecil Cook Davis, Clemson, S. C.; Mrs. Willis A. Godowns, Jr., Woodbury, Ga., and Mrs. Duane W. Fischer, Pine Mountain. There are 10 grandchildren.

# Phillips Retires As Mayor –
# Pine Mountain

*The Manchester Mercury*, March 29, 1962

Earl J. Phillips was mayor of Pine Mountain for a period of almost 10 years, ten years in which the town grew and many changes occurred.

By the time this paper reaches you this week, Pine Mountain will have elected a new mayor. Mr. Phillips did not seek reelection in this week's city election. I am sure that the citizens of the town join this writer in this special tribute to "Mr. Earl.", and in expressing appreciation to him for a job well done.

As mayor pro temp, Earl Jackson Phillips became mayor in 1952 upon the death in office of J. W. Caldwell, veteran city official. After serving Mr. Caldwell's unexpired term, Mr. Phillips ran for office and was elected in 1954, and in succeeding elections. Previously, he had served on the city council since 1945.

To say that Mayor Phillips is a busy man would be an understatement. In addition to fulfilling his duties as mayor and looking after his store, he is currently serving as president of the Chipley Development Corporation, chairman of the Harris County Board of Education, a trustee and member of the Board of Stewards of the Chipley Methodist Church, and is teacher of his Sunday School class.

The son of the late Olin and Jimmie Cummings Phillips, lifelong residents of this area, Mr. Phillips was born Feb. 10, 1911, on the family farm just east of the present city of Pine Mountain.

Following his graduation from Chipley High School, the well-known civic leader says, he worked one year at the town's first industry -- the ice plant -- before

*Photograph courtesy of Ibby Phillips Edgar*

**Earl Jackson Phillips**
**Feb. 10, 1911 – July 26, 2003**

entering the University of Georgia, where he received his degree in civil engineering in 1933.

He worked with government agencies, including the T.V.A., for a short while, then came back to Harris County in 1935 to work with the National Park Service at Roosevelt State Park. He was engineer for the construction of Liberty Bell Swimming Pool at historic King's Gap, and the Boy Scout Camp.

Mr. Earl says he threw away his instruments after being advised that the roads were "supposed to be rustic and not too straight."

He went back for his instruments however, for two years with the State Department and two years with the U. S. Army engineers at Moody Air Force Base at Valdosta before returning to Chipley where he opened his grocery business in 1944.

He is married to the former Miss Marion Douthit of Columbus. They have four children, a daughter, Isbel, who with her husband, Jim Edgar, recently moved from California to Pine Mountain for residence. The three sons are: Jack, a sophomore at the University of Georgia, Bob, a sophomore at Harris High, and Steve, a seventh grader at Chipley Elementary.

During his almost 10 years as mayor, Mr. Phillips has headed and completed a number of outstanding city improvement projects. To mention a few -- improvements were made in sewage and water systems, city lighting, maintenance, housing, streets, volunteer fire department and equipment and other areas.

The name of the town was changed, a new post office and depot secured, and the highway through the middle of town is to be straightened this springs.

A new industry moved into the building owned by the Chipley Development Corporation, and a citywide beautification program was begun with tourist attraction in mind.

This busy man has a hobby, farming on his old home place, and manages to find time to grow vegetables for his store. He also raises some beef and fattens a few porkers for his sausage-making. The sausage is in demand the year 'round in the meat department of the former mayor's grocery.

Mr. Earl is one of Pine Mountain's most enthusiastic "better home town" boosters, and has evidence throughout the city of a job "well done."

# Pine Mountain Train Depot

## Pine Mountain Depot Now in Operation
*The Pine Mountain Review*, 1962

The new Central of Georgia depot here is officially open for business. Office equipment was moved from the old building into the new structure during the weekend.

W. C. McLaney, local station agent, said that the new facility is very convenient, and even though the building is smaller than the old depot, there is plenty of room. The modern, functional structure houses an office, passenger waiting room, freight and express room and a rest room.

Mayor Earl J. Phillips said early this week that plans for moving the old building from the center of town have not been completed. The building will be sold to the highest bidder and Highway 27 through Pine Mountain will be straightened following removal of the old depot.

Local residents feel that the new depot, and removal of the old building, will add to the attractiveness of the town and will aid in enticing tourists to the area. Citizens of Pine Mountain and Harris County contributed toward constructions costs of the building.

## 'Treasures' Unearthed in Old Depot

Does D. F. White today rest in an unmarked grave somewhere in Georgia?

Or did his survivors know his headstone had become misplaced and order another?

These questions, and many others, were posed last week as workmen, dismantling Pine Mountain's "middle-of-the-road" railway depot, unearthed a veritable treasure trove of items in and under the building.

Topping the list was a head stone, and foot stone, bearing the inscription "D. F. White, Born 1845, Died 1911," discovered under the loading platform.

There were a number of old suitcases, some with clothing dating back to the early part of the century, and several old coins, one, a dime, bearing the date 1802.

All these items apparently will become property of William Harris and Roy Butts who bought the structure.

According to area residents the depot was built in 1908 or 1909 after a storm leveled the railway station.

The building is being torn down to clear the route for straightening U. S. Highway 27 and a new depot has been constructed some 300 yards south of the old site.


## Depot Schedules Announced May 1
*The Pine Mountain Review*, May 3, 1962

Beginning on Tuesday, May 1, one station agent will assume duties at depots in both Pine Mountain and Hamilton.

D.L. Trussell, Hamilton station master, will be transferred to a new location and W. C. McLaney who has served as agent in Pine Mountain for the past 13 years, will run offices in both towns.

McLaney will be at the Pine Mountain depot from 8 until 10 each morning, Monday through Friday, and at the Hamilton station from 10:15 a.m. until 4:45 p.m.

An opposite schedule of station service was originally proposed by railroad officials but was changed at a hearing before the Public Service Commission in Atlanta earlier this year. It was brought out that Hamilton has more revenue coming in to the station and shipped approximately 50 cars of pulp wood by rail each week. A delegation of Hamilton citizens attended the hearing.

McLaney reports that passengers boarding the Man O' War in Pine Mountain will secure tickets on the train. This is true for both departures, the 12:18 p.m. to Columbus and the 4:07 p.m. to Atlanta.

Express will not be handled on the train after May 1st but will be picked up at the Pine Mountain depot by truck in regular round-trip nightly runs from Columbus to Atlanta, McLaney said. This will be an advantage in that express can be picked up at the depot at 8 a.m. each morning, several hours earlier than former express arrivals by train.

The agent can be contacted by phone at either station by residents of both towns. There is no toll between Hamilton and Pine Mountain telephone exchanges.

## New Depot Step Toward Progress
*The Pine Mountain Review*, July 1, 1965

The citizens of Pine Mountain believe that the new, smaller and more functional depot erected in the spring of 1962 has made the town more attractive.

Removal of the old depot from the center of town was a step toward progress. Beautification and attractiveness of the city has been emphasized since the livelihood of the area is changing from agriculture to tourist attraction.

Because of the proximity of Pine Mountain to the Callaway Gardens, Roosevelt State Park and Warm Springs, visitors in the little town have increased.

Since the old middle-of-the-road depot has been removed, U. S. Highway 27 now runs straight through Pine Mountain. The new portion of the highway runs adjacent to the railroad tracks, leaving room on the opposite side for diagonal parking as well as a new sidewalk and curb along the East side of the highway in front of the business establishments.

The new depot was made possible through the combined efforts of the citizens of Harris County in cooperation with the Central of Georgia Railroad. A contribution toward construction of the building was made by the Ida Cason Callaway Foundation, the purchase of the right-of-way was made by the county commissioners, and the installation of water and sewage facilities was made by the Town of Pine Mountain.

The railroad through Chipley (now Pine Mountain) began as a project started by William Dudley Chipley, Columbus native, following the War Between the States. The narrow gauge line was constructed a few miles at the time, as funds and materials became available, with Rome, Ga., as the termination point.

The rail line came to a halt at Kingsboro (now Cataula) near Mulberry Grove, and was later completed to Hamilton. Sometime around 1875 the tracks pushed on to Summit, known today as Tip Top, and before 1880 were completed to a community site later called Old Hood. Old Hood residents were those that moved from the King's Gap Village which had built up around the stage coach stop, according to senior residents of Pine Mountain.

Due to a defect in the land title at Old Hood, W. D. Chipley chose a spot about a mile further north to build the station, which he named for himself. Again, the residents moved.

It was several years before the railway was extended northward from Chipley. A turntable was erected at the northern end of the business district of the little town and the train made daily trips to and from Columbus.

The first steam engine used on the routes was the "Estes," replaced a few years later by the "Pine Mountain," and still later by the "Big 4."

The first station master at the Chipley depot was Marshall Dixon. The present station master, W. C. McLaney, took D. C. Royal Sr.'s place in 1948 when Royal retired because of illness following 24 years of service.

The tracks were changed to wide gauge in 1908, the same year a storm blew away most of the town, including the depot, Baptist church, the hotel and nearly 40 homes.

The old middle-of-the-road depot was constructed the following year and was used continuously until torn down in 1962.

The name of the town was changed from Chipley to Pine Mountain in February 1958. This name change was made "to help identify the town with the nearby recreational facilities," one town official said.

# Dr. John E. Champion Named Vice-President of F.S.U.

*The Manchester Mercury*, August 9, 1962

Dr. John Elmer Champion, son of Mr. and Mrs. Jesse H. Champion of Pine Mountain, has accepted the position of vice-president of Florida State University at Tallahassee, Fla. He will assume the post on Sept. 1.

Champion, 40-year-old native of Pine Mountain, has been a member of the FSU faculty since 1956. He succeeds Dr. Milton W. Carothers who resigned as vice-president in order to devote full time to teaching.

In announcing the change, President Gordon W. Blackwell said, "We are extremely fortunate that Dr. John E. Champion, who has served as professor and assistant dean in the School of Business, will succeed Dr. Carothers. Dr. Champion's demonstrated abilities in management and fiscal affairs mean that he is specially qualified to serve as vice-president for administration."

Champion holds bachelor's and master's degrees from the University of Georgia and a Ph.D. degree from the University of Michigan. He taught at the University of Georgia before joining the faculty at F.S.U.

He and a fellow faculty member, Dr. Homer A. Black, are the authors of a textbook, "Accounting in Business Decisions," which is widely used in American universities.

Dr. Champion, a graduate of Chipley High School, Class of '39, served in the Pacific theatre during World War II. He is married to the former Mary Lanier of West Point. They have two children, Sally, 6, and Johnny, 4.

*Note by Mrs. Champion, 2008: John E. Champion, one of my classmates in the 1939 class of Chipley High School, became president of F.S.U. A group of us from Pine Mountain attended his inauguration. The event was covered by reporters and photographers from throughout this area. I did not have a chance to file a story at that time.*

# Work on "27" is Completed

*The Columbus Enquirer,* November 1, 1962

U.S. Highway 27 now runs straight through Pine Mountain. Surfacing of the road across the site of the old depot has been completed. A new center line has been painted and the traffic light is expected to be relocated this week, according to O. E. White, Pine Mountain mayor.

The new portion of the highway runs adjacent to the railroad tracks, leaving room on the opposite side for diagonal parking in front of Phillips-Douthit, Marshall Furniture Co., Hall's Service Station, Middlebrook's Barber Shop, and Wisdom Motor Company.

Mayor White met with state highway officials in Atlanta recently to discuss the possibility of running a sidewalk and curb along the East side of the highway in front of the business establishments.

# Pine Mountain Elects
# City Councilmen, Mayor

*The Columbus Enquirer*, 1962

Local voters Wednesday elected two city councilmen and a mayor who will oversee administration of the city or the next two years.

According to Mrs. Mary Askew, city clerk, 234 votes were cast in an election which saw former Councilman O. E. White assume the mayor's seat, and incumbent A. H. (Buck) Anderson, and Vance Smith, Sr., elected to the council. White, with 125 votes, succeeds former Mayor Earl Phillips, who has held the post since 1952.

Anderson, who also serves as a member of the Harris County Commission, is a partner in an auto repair firm here. He polled 146 votes.

Smith, who operates for lease a fleet of heavy machinery equipment, polled 206 votes, more than any candidate.

In the race for mayor, Tom Livingston ran second with 83 votes; C. E. Woodruff was third with 16, and Talmadge Williams received six votes. A third candidate for two seats on the council, Lee Murphy, polled 77 votes.

The new mayor, a former dairyman and feed store owner, operates a poultry business in Harris County. He is a past president of the Pine Mountain Chamber of Commerce and a long-time civic leader.

# Harold ("Tobe") Magruder

## Magruder Becomes a Celebrity
*The Columbus Enquirer*, December 13, 1962

Harold (Mr. Tobe) Magruder, 90-year-old resident of Pine Mountain, has become a celebrity. The active senior citizen is getting quite a kick from the fan mail he is receiving from various parts of the nation.

It started when a recent article about Mr. Tobe's gardening activities was sent out by the Associated Press to newspapers throughout the United States.

A lady in Bluefield, W. Va., said she saw the article in her local paper and requested some tips on flowers or gardening from Mr. Tobe. She wrote, "I am a widow and love flowers. I would like to know more about them." She added that she guessed it would soon be time in Georgia to be thinking about gardening.

A clipping from New Orleans arrived with the following note to Mr. Tobe: "I saw in the Sunday Times Picayune where you give flowers to people in Pine Mountain. You are making folks happy with your flowers. My mother used to say, 'give flowers while one is living.' God will bless you. Your family must be proud of you. Congratulations and may you have lots more birthdays."

A man in Schenectady, N.Y., sent a card to be autographed by Mr. Tobe. He wrote that he is endeavoring to acquire autographs of persons in the United States who have reached their 90th birthday. He added that obtaining Mr. Tobe's autograph would add greatly to his endeavor.

A letter postmarked near the Canada border was from a lady who stated that she read the article in the Bismarck (North Dakota) Tribune on Nov. 26. She wrote: "Dear Harold Magruder, Congratulations to you for the wonderful things you are doing in your community. Wish there were more people like you. What a wonderful world this would be!"

Mr. Tobe, who does not need glasses for reading, says he hasn't answered all the letters yet. However, he has composed a few lines of poetry that may be used to send to his "pen pals."

He said that "he feels the weight of his years and his back sometimes is bent, but his get up and go hasn't got up and went -- yet. He added that in looking back over his four score and ten years he counts (like the sun dial) only the shining hours.

The spry gentleman said that he transferred from Alabama Polytechnic Institute (now Auburn University) in 1891 to Life's University of Hard Knocks. "I took the full course," he said, "majoring in all the antics of Fickle Fortune, Chance and Circumstance."

"I graduated from this school at the end of the fall term, 1960" (when he retired from his farming interests), he said. "I think I deserved a diploma, but there was no one around to conduct the ceremony"

"Now I am content to sit and watch the world go by," he added.

Mr. Tobe really does not sit around. He continues to grow his flowers, as the original article stated, and gives them away to local organizations and individuals.

He is very proud of his five year drivers license and his car -- a big yellow Cadillac.

He loves young people and enjoys making them happy with little remembrances. His hobby, he says, is 38 great nieces and nephews -- to whom he is most dedicated.

The last time I talked to Mr. Tobe he was making plans to go over to Auburn University to see a group of coeds who wanted to meet a 90-year-old-man. They are the sorority sisters of one of his great nieces.

## Mr. Tobe Succumbs at Age Ninety-Two
*The Harris County Journal*, January 14, 1965

Harold (Mr. Tobe) Magruder, 92, died at his residence in Pine Mountain Friday morning, January 1, following an illness of several months.

Mr. Tobe was born in Meriwether County near Pine Mt. and lived in Pine Mt. most of his life. He attended Auburn University in 1891 and operated the first Ford agency in Pine Mt. He also operated a soft drink bottling company for a short time and later was a salesman for farm machinery. He was engaged in farming in this area for a period of 70 years.

On his 90th birthday, Mr. Tobe was featured in a news story sent to papers throughout the nation by the Associated Press. He became a celebrity when letters began pouring in from persons interested in a 90-year-old flower gardener who gave away his flowers to schools, organizations, shut-ins and individuals. Mr. Tobe with his basket of flowers was a familiar figure in Pine Mountain. He carried a five-year drivers license and drove his yellow Cadillac until last August.

Funeral was held Saturday afternoon at Chipley Methodist Church with the Rev. Charles Clarke, pastor, officiating. Burial was in Pine Mountain Cemetery.

Mr. Tobe had no immediate family but is survived by 19 nieces and nephews and a number of great-nieces and nephews.

# Farmers Tour Electric Cotton Gin

*The Columbus Enquirer*, September 17, 1964

"Although cotton is no longer king in Harris County, it is a major factor in our economy."

This comment was made by Forest Salter, Harris County agent, Monday during open house at Dunn's new all-electric cotton gin.

Maynard Dunn, who has been in the ginning business here 22 years, has replaced diesel machinery with modern electric equipment. The plant is the only commercial electric gin in the area. Dunn expects to gin 2,500 bales this season.

Farmers from Harris, Troup, Meriwether and surrounding counties toured the gin to view the operation of the new equipment.

At noon, the farmers were guests of Mr. and Mrs. Dunn for a barbecue.

In a short talk after the meal, Salter said Dunn is in a key position to bring the farmer more for his crop.

"Better ginning equipment means a better-quality bale," Salter said. "This gives the farmer better prices."

Salter said the cotton crop in Harris County is good in spite of excessive rain at planting time and in increase in the insect population. Due to the rain, insecticides are not as effective, he explained.

Harris County's cotton allotment was 1,500 acres, and approximately 1,000 acres were planted, Salter said.

The county agent listed ways which cotton stimulates the economy. He said industries boosted by cotton include lime and fertilizer, farm machinery and equipment, transportation, warehousing and storage and feed and oil. Insecticides boost the chemical industry, he said.

Salter also mentioned that Pine Mountain's only industry, a clothing-manufacturing plant, and the textile mills in neighboring cities, also are dependent on cotton production.

Guests at the meeting included Charles Campbell, field engineer, Columbus Cotton Gin Co.; Charles Lumpkin, Rome Oil Mill; Harold Lummus, Jr., R. L. Drew and G. E. Leonard, officials of Lummus Cotton Gin Co., Columbus; Richard Thompson, representing Citizens and Southern Bank, LaGrange, and Roy Askew, Farmers and Merchants Bank president here.

# Cason Callaway Biography is Fascinating Book on Georgian

*The Columbus Enquirer*, December 10, 1964

"Cason Callaway of Blue Springs," is a fascinating biography of an outstanding Georgian who lived in and loved Harris County.

Mrs. Callaway was hostess for a group of family friends, the news media and representatives of the textile trade press, for a preview of the book Friday afternoon at her home.

Also present were representatives of the two LaGrange libraries and the Bradley Memorial Library of Columbus. Mrs. Chip Roberts of Atlanta and Washington, D. C., was a special guest.

The biography is the work of Paul Schubert of Shell, Wyo., a close friend of the Callaway family.

Mr. Schubert writes in an engaging and readable style. He presents a warm and intimate description of Mr. Callaway's home life and personal friendships, together with a comprehensive account of his business accomplishments and civic and philanthropic activities.

Mr. Cason was a textile magnate, a director of U. S. Steel and other important corporations, a Regent of the University System of Georgia and, last but not least, a successful farmer.

The word "farmer" only partially describes Mr. Cason's relation to the soil, Schubert points out. As a "farmer" he became interested in feeding people's bodies. Later he extended this to an interest in feeding their souls – thus the development of Ida Cason Callaway Gardens.

Many changes took place in the lives of Mr. Cason and his family after he purchased Blue Springs in 1930. Those changes were small compared to those he made on

Harris County hills and streams. Fulfillment of his dream is a gift of beauty to us – his friends and neighbors.

-------------------------❖----------------------------

*Note by Mrs. Champion, 2008: I "poured" coffee for Mrs. Callaway that day, and received a copy of the book inscribed with a personal note from Mrs. Callaway.*

# Brick Building Houses
# Chipley Grammar School

*The Pine Mountain Review*, July 1, 1965

Pine Mountain boasts a modern, attractive red brick building for the eight grades at Chipley Elementary School.

An addition, consisting of two class rooms, cafetorium, administrative unit and rest rooms, was completed in April 1962.

The existing building, formerly Chipley High School, was renovated with new ceiling and tile floors. Total cost of the new addition and renovation totaled $85,163.28.

The former elementary school building, a two-story structure, was torn down upon completion of the new building.

The school has paved drive ways and well-kept playgrounds. The Parent-Teacher Association assisted in landscaping the school campus and obtaining playground equipment.

Earlier this year, a new sliding board, jungle gym and maypole swing was added by a community fund-raising drive sponsored by the P.T.A.

A well-stocked library is maintained at the school. New books have been added during the past three years through the school, organizations, and generosity of friends.

# Former School Bus Driver Recalls Three Decades of Harris Service

*The Columbus Enquirer*, October 7, 1965

Sim King has given up his school bus route after 32 years of service.

"School bus drivers don't 'retire,' they just give up their routes," King said.

He will devote full time to his job with the local Standard Oil agency.

King began driving a school bus here in 1933 at the age of 21. He had dropped out of school when he finished the seventh grade and decided to go back to classes when he began driving the bus. He finished Chipley High School in three years and later married Virginia Hadley, a member of his graduating class.

His first school bus had a homemade body, plank benches for seats and canvas curtains on the sides to keep out the weather. The first year he transported 20 students, both elementary and high school pupils, over 10 miles of dirt roads in the King's Gap area.

"The roads were bad in wet weather," King said. "I remember one afternoon I left the bus in the mud and walked home."

King made his last run a few days ago in a modern bus carrying 38 students. His route covered 56 miles of paved and improved roads.

"I've seen a great change in the roads during the past 32 years," he said.

The veteran bus driver chuckled as he recalled some of the "Class Trips" made in one of his early buses.

"We went to Florida several times and to Chattanooga," he recalled. "Miss Janie O'Neal (one of the high-school faculty members) was the class-trip director and carried her rocking chair along on the bus so she could ride in comfort. Once in Chattanooga I made a sudden stop at a traffic light, and Miss Janie and her chair flipped over backwards."

King explained that he enjoyed his bus route.

"I had some of the best children," he said. "And some of the worst.

"It took a lot of paddling and a lot of loving to maintain discipline, but I never had to put a child off the bus for misbehavior," he said. "If you can get the child to like you, you can control him"

"I had to wrap cut fingers and sore toes, wipe faces and give aspirin," King said.

"Sometimes I had to stop the bus to help farmers put up cows and pigs that had wandered into the road."

"It was quite an experience, being out early in the morning. You could get a good look at what had happened during the night – how much it rained, the amount of frost, etc."

During the past decade, both elementary and high school students boarded Sim King's bus on the King's Gap route to Chipley Elementary School, but the high school pupils changed to another bus for the trip to Harris County High at Hamilton. They returned to Chipley Elementary in the afternoon and were picked up by King for the ride home.

Two generations of students were King's passengers. His own children were among the first to board the bus each morning. One of his sons, Wayne, is in the Army, stationed at Fort Knox; another son, Warren, is married and lives in LaGrange, and the daughter, Ginny, is a 1965 graduate of Harris County High School. The youngest child, Ray, is a sixth-grader at Chipley Elementary.

King said that he will miss the school children and the daily trips, but there is one thing that "he will look back on with a great deal of pride": In the 32 years he had an accident-free record. Not a single child was injured on the bus. Franklin Davenport of Pine Mountain will replace King on the King's Gap route.

# Fire Destroys Roosevelt Church

*The Columbus Enquirer*, April 15, 1967

Roosevelt Memorial Church – the only church to which the late President Franklin D. Roosevelt gave written permission to use his name – was destroyed by fire late Thursday.

The wood frame building, constructed in the shape of a cross, was dedicated on Nov. 5, 1942, some nine years after Roosevelt wrote W. T. (Tap) Bennett, giving the interdenominational church permission to use his name.

Roosevelt wrote: "Thank you ever so much for that grand little note you sent me on May 13 (1933) advising me of the desire of the congregation of the new community church of Pine Mountain Valley to name their new church in my honor.

"I am deeply touched by the thoughtfulness of the members of the congregation and shall feel greatly honored to have the new community church bear my name."

A framed photostat of the letter was hung in the church foyer, and officials at first thought the original copy had been destroyed. However, it was learned that the original was on loan to the Little White House at Warm Springs.

The fire was discovered about 9 p.m. Thursday by Mrs. Jimmy C. Jones as she was driving past the sanctuary. She went to a nearby service station and summoned H. M. Wemmer, who grabbed a fire extinguisher and ran to the building, only to discover that the entire sanctuary was engulfed in flames.

Destroyed in the fire was the Rev. Harold Bennett's 500-volume library and copies of his sermons.

Mrs. Owen Riley, Sunday School superintendent, Friday said members were busy getting the annex ready for

*Photograph courtesy of Roosevelt Memorial Church*

**Roosevelt Memorial Church**
**Pine Mountain Valley, Georgia**

Sunday services. The annex, a separate building, was not damaged.

She noted that the insurance on the church will "by no means" cover the loss. She emphasized that the members will rebuild the church.

Members also built the original church. Officials noted that many of them contributed materials and worked on the structure, which was first started in 1938 and completed in 1942.

President Roosevelt, who was visiting in Warm Springs, was unable to attend the dedication on Nov. 5, because of illness.

# Pine Mountain Area Folks Tell of Days Before REA Came

*The Columbus Enquirer*

"Many were the times I stuck an Irish potato over the opening in the top of a gallon kerosene can," she said. "Before electricity brought lights to the rural Valley area, the county store had to keep in a large supply of oil, lam wicks and chimneys."

In reminiscing about "the good ole days" before REA, Mrs. W. C. Teaver, "Miss Mattie Pope" to everyone in the Salem community near Pine Mountain, recalled the big "icebox" at her little store that was forever running out of ice and the gasoline tank that had to be pumped by hand.

The well in the store yard still furnishes a mighty refreshing drink and there's something about letting down the bucket and drawing it back up that makes the water taste just a little bit better but gone are the days of "tottin' water."

Lewis Bryant, Troup Electric Membership Co-op director and a Salem community dairyman, barely recalls an old cream separator used by his parents, a Master Farm Family, as he goes about milking with the modern pipeline process in operation on the farm today.

Ulver Perdue's workshop and poultry houses are quite a contrast to pre-REA days and cabinets constructed in the shop have turned the Perdue's kitchen into a picture right out of a magazine. Little resemblance to the room with the wood stove, the water bucket and the washtub can be found in farm homes in the area today.

Little country churches have removed all evidence of lamps with shiny reflectors from the walls and melodies from modern electric organs require less effort than the old pedal models. Old-timers, and some not so old, remember when young gentlemen help out in "pedaling" when long song services proved a bit tiring for a pretty organist.

A number of the members of Bethany Baptist Church, just west of Pine Mountain, vividly recall the night that electricity came to their church. The Rev. A. L. Phillips was conducting a revival meeting the first week in August, a short time following installation of REA lines along the main roads in the area.

The Rev. Mr. Phillips made the statement that the church could have lights before the week was out if the people really wanted them. Contributions poured in. There was not enough time for wiring the church or getting the poles up, nevertheless, there was light in the church during the Friday night service. A single naked bulb glowed at the end of a long extension cord, which was plugged into an outlet in Fred Champion's newly wired chicken house across the field.

Old small schoolhouses, no longer needed for educational purposed because of consolidation, have been turned into community recreation centers. Electrical equipment is used in cooking and sewing demonstrations, in craft workshops, in musical programs and other activities.

More than 6,000 farms and homes in Troup, Harris, Muscogee and Heard Counties in Georgia and Chambers County, Ala., are using electricity today from the Troup Electric Membership Co-op which was organized at the courthouse in LaGrange July 10, 1936, a little more than a year after President Roosevelt signed the executive order establishing REA.

Charter members of the Co-op from Salem and other communities recall how they went from room to room flipping on light switches. "We couldn't afford switches," one couple commented. "We pulled strings on dangling drop cords."

"I wish we could record some of the conversations that take place each year at our annual meetings," said Miss Louise Prickett, Co-op home economist. Some of the silvery haired grandmothers often tell modern young mothers that they should feel awfully lucky to have washers, dryers, and other labor saving devices in their homes today. "We raised eight children before we got electricity," said one gracious lady.

Mrs. Prickett and her green station wagon have become a familiar sight to home owners throughout the area as she goes from one community to another assisting with lighting problems and lending a helping hand in planning new kitchen or remodeling old ones.

Perhaps the one person who really knows just how much the area has changed since "light came to the Valley" is O. R. Caudle who has served on the board of directors of the Troup Co-op since the organizational meeting. He has served as secretary-treasurer since Aug. 1937, and one of the things he enjoys most is going out at various times during the year to read meters. "That's when I have a chance to observe progress on the farms and in rural industries," he said.

He told about the "grass incubator" on James Trammell's farm near Pine Mountain that produces oats for his dairy herd.

# Chipley Native, Known as Poet, Dies in Arkansas

*The Columbus Enquirer*

R. E. Bowles, 83, native of Chipley (now Pine Mountain), died Sunday in a Texarkana hospital and funeral services were held Tuesday in Foreman, Ark., where he had made his home for the past 30 years.

Mr. Bowles was the brother of the late A. C. and W. H. Bowles of Pine Mountain and made numerous visits here to relatives and friends in his hometown. He was the author of two books of poems, many of which recalled experiences in Chipley, Harris County and the mountain.

In his poem entitled "About Chipley" he wrote:

Georgia skies are bluer,
Friends are truer
The sun shines the brightest
The moon and the stars ever shining
Hears never, never pining
Where sorrows and cares are lightest
About Chipley

Under the trees on the mountain
The water spouts and sprays from the fountain
The lakes reflect the beauties around
Of the oaks, the chestnuts and stately pine trees
With the ever-constant humming of the bees
And where songs of the birds abound
About Chipley.

While visiting here one summer he wrote:

This road seems so strange
This road to LaGrange
Unlike the road we once traveled on
The valleys not so shrunken and low
The hills not so high and steep
I Know
Longcane is smaller
So is Blue John
Neither is Big Creek so big and deep
Nor is the hill beyond so long and steep.

He composed poems about the old homestead, the old mill, the rocky comfort of the old town, the trees and the birds. He wrote lines about his relatives and friends, and verses describing his "mute" friends, including Hig, his dog, Billie, his saddle horse, and Old Mrs. Yellow, his cat.

In the early stage of the Ida Cason Callaway Gardens development he wrote:

What, is this a new day?
With the Pine Mountain's upheaval
With your means, ingenuity, your dreams, Mr. Callaway
Changing this beautiful mountain's forest primeval.

The enchanting lake with its sandy beaches
Watered by spring and fountain
From its remote reaches
Adown and along the sides of Pine Mountain

Magnificent gardens with flowers manifold
Sweet aroma of wild honeysuckle, sweet shrubs, blending
With your rose, rhododendrons, hibiscus, hyacinths, marigold
A beautifully adorned panorama unending.

Foot-paths, cow trails changing
To well-paved and polished highways
The whole landscape rearranging
The mountain, nevertheless enhancing always.

Improvement, multitude developments made
The whole terrain renovated to this new day
To you, the benefactor, to you our sincerest accolade
To you congratulations, Mr. Callaway.

# Lil's Lobby ... Hobbies
*The Pine Mountain Review*

This week's guest in our hobby lobby was suggested by not one person but by several. Malinda Brooks has an unusual hobby in that she does not collect things for her own pleasure but enjoys giving happiness to others. She sends numerous greeting cards to friends and acquaintances, even to those she knows as fellow citizens of our town.

Malinda began her hobby before she started to school by drawing valentines and making get-well cards. She has no idea how many she has mailed in the past ten years but according to reports from just about everyone in town the number must be tremendous.

Malinda is a senior at Harris High, a member of the Beta Club, Tri-Hi-Y, and Latin Club. In addition to her hobby of sending cards, she loves children and enjoys working with the nursery department at the Chipley Methodist Church.

She plans to enroll in La Grange College in June to begin her studies in preparation for a teaching career.

# Uncle Billy Was a 'Character'

*The Pine Mountain Review*

*The Pine Mountain Review editor's note: The death of W. M. "Uncle Billy" Whitehead, 90, one of Chipley's oldest colored people is being marked by his white friends as well as his colored friends. He has been one of the "landmarks" of Chipley and a paper written on him by Mrs. Hubert Champion has been brought to our attention and it is most interesting and we would like to have you read it. This was written ten years ago by Mrs. Champion when she was trying to find information about her grandfather who was a Confederate veteran.*

One day I happened to think about an old Negro man in Chipley by the name of Billy Whitehead, whose father was a slave on the Whitehead plantation near my grandfather's farm south of Chipley. My grandfather's first wife was Mary Frances Whitehead who died quite young and when I called on "Uncle Billy" he assured me that she was from the same family that had owned his father as a slave. Uncle Billy was born the year the War Between the States ended. He remembered my grandfather but "disremembered" what he looked like.

"Uncle Billy" is quite a character around Chipley. I spent most of the morning talking with him and I became so interested in him that I almost forgot about my grandfather.

"Uncle Billy" plays several musical instruments and has the most amusing contraption made of odds and ends. It resembles a combination of Spike Jones' band and a puppet show. He has rigged up parts of an old sewing machine in such a way that when he pedals with his foot some little dolls on the table top do all sorts of crazy things. "Joe Lewis" dances, kicking his feet way out. "Aunt Dinnah" sits in a little home-made chair and churns away.

Her little churn dasher keeps perfect time with the music. A little fiddler saws back and forth as "Uncle Billy" pedals. He made the dolls out of scraps of wood. "Aunt Dinnah" has a head from some child's discarded doll. "Uncle Billy" made the clothes, too, gay little red jackets, black trousers, covered buttons and all. "Aunt Dinnah" wears a long-sleeved black dress, a white apron and a white ruffled cap. The faces on "Joe Lewis" and the fiddler are cut from a magazine and pasted in place. "Uncle Billy" can change their faces whenever he wishes.

While the dolls are going through their paces, "Uncle Billy" is picking a guitar, blowing a funny looking horn that's held in place on a special little stand, beating the drums with one foot and pedaling with the other. Sometimes he substitutes a "harp" for the horn. At the moment he thinks most appropriate he suddenly pulls a string and bells start ringing.

Children around Chipley like to invite "Uncle Billy" to their birthday parties, and he just loves to go to entertain them. He told me that some people came all the way from Mountville (about twenty miles from Chipley) one Sunday afternoon just to hear him play.

"Uncle Billy" makes up most of the songs he sings, but he can revise any of the old favorites to suit the occasion. His most famous song is his version of the "Ballad of the Boll Weevil." I asked him if he would sing it for me and let me write it as he sang. He said that he would be glad to, but he thought "it would be better if we had one of them there typewriter things so I could write real fast." I assured him that i could write with my pen much faster than I could with a typewriter, especially with my style of typing, so he started singing:

You run 'round here last fall --
Select out your cotton seed,
And when they come up --

127

They grows just like a weed.
Stalks grow high --
Limbs grow wide,
Go anywhere in the cotton and
Lay down and hide.
I pull up one them fine stalks cotton,
Brung it to town,
Mr. Kimbrough he comes out
And he's a lookin' a-round. (This has reference to the
Kimbrough Brothers' General Store.)
He looks at the stalk, the leaves and the boll.
"Come here, Haywood," he say,
"Here where a weevil have punched a hole."
Mr. Haywood he come out
And he look at the boll.
He say, "Henry, lets you and me
Go on back in the store,
"Cause I doubt if'n us can let
The farmers have much more."

At this point "Uncle Billy" sung a verse about the
hard times the farmers had after they lost their cotton. The
verse ended with something about the Korean War, but
"Uncle Billy" suggested that I leave out that verse since the
boll weevil was the cause of this particular trouble. He
continued the song with the conversation between the boll
weevil and the rain:

The rain say, "Mr. Weevil,
You is might smart, I'm told,
But if'n it weren't for my water
You wouldn't have no boll."
"Excuse me, Mr. Rain,
I knowed I's too fast,
But I gotta get this here cotton
That's growing in de grass.

Mr. Rain, you just take care the
Blossom, I'll tend to the boll,
And there won't be no cotton
Picking when the weather gets cold."

Another verse told about the boll weevil chasing a rabbit and ended with the following little rhyme:

The Weevil thought that
Rabbit's tail was a boll of cotton
That he had stole sometime last night,
And he says, "Mr. Rabbit, if I
Catch you with a green one,
Us is going to have a Fight."

"Uncle Billy" said that there were several other verses but he "disremembered" them. He was most anxious for me to make a copy of his latest poem about the Georgia sales tax. It goes like this:

Mr. Herman Talmadge, he sets
Up yonder in his fine arm chair.
Looking for every copper that
Belongs to him to come up there.
He says, "Boy, if'n I find out you done slipped out some
Them coppers to buy whiskey and beers,
I's going to help the courts send you to the pen
From fifteen to twenty years.

I took some pictures of "Uncle Billy" with my son's midget flash camera. He noticed the sign I had made on a little slate I picked up in his little house. In it I had written, "Uncle Billy's One Man Band." "Miss Lillian," he said, "when you gets them pictures back you write 'Whitehead' on that sign so they'll know which Billy I is." He is very proud of his name  The first thing you notice when you see his neat little white cottage is the name plate on the front door, "Wm. WHITEHEAD" it reads -- in silver letters.

As I was leaving he noticed the ball-point pen in my hand.

"Miss Lillian," he asked, "Is that a ink pen you got there?"

I explained that it was a ball-pen and showed him how it worked. He said that he had one like it but that "he couldn't find no place to put the ink in at."

I took his pen, pressed the end opposite the point and the point popped out. I made a few marks with it and then handed it to him. He scribbled a little and looked up at me.

"Miss Lillian," he said, "it's a miracle, ain't it?"

A miracle, I thought as I drove homeward. Oh, "Uncle Billy," wouldn't it be a miracle if some day we find our story in print, and who knows, maybe somebody, somewhere, can tell us something about my grandfather.

*Note by Mrs. Champion, 2008: My grandfather died in Harris County, Ga., when my father was only a week old. Years later a family visiting relatives in Columbus came to Pine Mountain and noticed the name 'Dismuke's' on one of the store fronts next to Dr. Ellis' office downtown. That family was descended from B. W. Dismukes, Sr., and Mary Frances Whitehead. They gave me the Dismukes family history and sent a photograph of my grandfather when they got back to their home in Dallas, Texas.*

# Dairyman's Daughter Steals the Limelight

*The Columbus Enquirer*

The modern farmer's daughter is stealing the limelight from the registered cattle, prizewinning permanent pastures, and highly productive crops.

Minus the daily chore with the old milk pail, the dairyman's daughter turns to more interesting thoughts of "keeping 'em happy down on the farm."

Little Pamela Avery, 10-year-old daughter of Mr. and Mrs. Curtis Avery, Jr., a Harris County Master Farm Family who live near Pine Mountain, finds farm life exciting. She adds quite a bit of excitement herself with her singing and dancing talents.

Pam represented Harris County as a Hi-Neighbor queen in the recent Christmas parade. She has participated in numerous talent shows in the area and recently appeared on television with the Harris County 4-H Club group.

An active 4-H member at Mountain Hill School in Harris County, where she is in the fourth grade, Pam lists her projects, in addition to talent, as health, childcare and dairying.

Mrs. Avery, who serves as 4-H advisor, accompanies Pam on the piano.

# Dr. Ray E. Watford Opens Office for Practice of Chiropractic

*The Columbus Enquirer*

Dr. Ray E. Watford, Chiropractor, has located in Pine Mountain in the office building formerly occupied by Dr. W. P. Ellis.

Dr. Watford spent last week washing windows and getting the office ready for opening this week.

To the ordinary person these tasks are merely routine, but Dr. Watford is no ordinary person. He is blind.

He describes his world of darkness as a nuisance, not a handicap.

In Sept., 1950, he was on the front lines in Korea, as an observer in a forward outpost. The enemy launched a surprise attack and overran his position. A hand grenade exploded in his face. His sight was gone, but not his courage.

Overlooked by the charging Reds, Watford was picked up by the medics without ever losing consciousness. He was in Brooke Army Hospital in San Antonio, Texas, for six months. He then went to Hines Veterans Hospital in Chicago and was assigned to the rehabilitation center. He learned Braille, the use of a cane, and other aids for the blind, but he wasn't content to live an average blind man's existence.

He had quit high school to enter the Army. He completed his high school course at night while working days. Then he entered Logan Chiropractic College of St. Louis, Mo., and graduated fifth in his class, 10 years to the month after he was wounded in Korea.

He was among the first of a very few to pass Alabama's Basic Science Board established by law in Jan., 1960.

A native of Houston County, Ala., Watford was reared in Columbus. His parents, Mr. and Mrs. Elton Watford reside there at the present time.

Dr. Watford began his private practice in Columbus. Later he was associated with practitioners in Phenix City, and with Dr. Joseph H. Liles, in Opelika.

It is difficult to detect that Dr. Watford is blind. He looks a person straight in the eye during a conversation. He has amazing memory of voices and greets his newfound Pine Mountain friends by name.

He says that it is not difficult to locate old bone breaks or muscular disturbances through his fingertips.

The chiropractor is married to the former Ruth Moye of Pine Mountain, and has three children. They reside in Pine Mountain in the former John Owing's residence. They attend First Baptist Church here.

# Little Gem of the Mountain

*The Columbus Ledger-Enquirer Sunday Magazine*

Although Columbus took the top honors in the statewide "Stay and See Georgia" contest, nearby Pine Mountain took its share of glory, too. Residents there painted and planted their way to top place in Class Five of the competition.

A cleanup and beautification program was started several years ago when Pine Mountain was a dying community named Chipley. Citizens accomplished a lot then, but the tourist promotion campaign gave them new interest in completing community projects. The results of Pine Mountain's "Stay and See" efforts have produced a more modern and attractive community as well as a contest winner.

A transformation in the business area of the town, along U. S. 27, is being noted by returning tourists. Freshly painted and modernized store fronts and a bright array of flowers in planters along the streets present a "new look" and reflect the pride of the townspeople.

William H. (Billy) Kimbrough, local merchant and civic leader, served as general chairman for Pine Mountain's participation in the "Stay and See" program.

He stated that Pine Mountain's award is the result of cooperation of the whole town in the cleanup and beautification projects. Merchants and residents went all-out to paint up, fix up and beautify surroundings with planting of flowers, shrubs and trees.

Large numbers of magnolia trees were contributed by the Ida Cason Callaway Gardens and distributed to home owners and businesses.

O.E. White, mayor, headed the cleanup and beautification committee. The city purchased a tractor and grass mower and increased the city garbage cleanup service.

The Chipley Woman's Club, headed by Mrs. Fletcher Chapman, Sr. took on the project of planting flowers in boxes and planters along the city streets. They also encouraged home owners in beautification projects.

Mary George Hixon, Negro community leader, was asked by the Woman's Club to head cleanup and beautification projects around homes in the Negro residential areas. She also headed distribution of magnolia trees in that area.

One by one Pine Mountain business owners knocked out their store fronts and replaced them with new glass and brick exteriors. The modernization process extended to interiors with new lighting and redecorating. A wider variety of goods was stocked, and customer convenience was emphasized.

Preston Gill, restaurant owner, headed the hospitality committee and distributed leaflets on how to treat tourists.

"A healthy attitude of residents toward strangers is of vital importance," he pointed out. "We've got to keep them happy if we want them to come, see, spend and come again."

# From Cows to Catfish and Collards

February 1974

First Person Editor
C/O *The Reader's Digest*
Pleasantville, NY 10570

Dear Mr. First Person Editor:

You won't believe this (if I had time to think about it, I wouldn't believe it either) but I am asking you to hurry and send my rejected "LETTER TO THE EDITOR" back to me -- I sent you the necessary stamped envelope.

You see -- that letter WAS written on the spur of the moment, and I really didn't have but one sheet of paper. It was all TOO TRUE. Doug Wallace and Charlie Black are real people -- they really did help me with those news stories and photos and they really were printed in *The Columbus (GA) Enquirer*. Charlie is now Associate Editor of the Enquirer and Doug is a well-known TV personality here in our part of Georgia. I don't think they would mind my using their names but I guess I SHOULD get their permission, shouldn't I? (It is awfully presumptuous of me to think that you would even consider publishing that letter, isn't it?) Also, I didn't mean to imply that the Enquirer's Sunday Magazine was low on funds -- THEY DEFINITELY ARE NOT -- I was shooting features to them so regularly (and so fast) that the editor was trying to tell me in a nice way that they wanted to share their budget with other writers. I was about to run out of neighbors with pickles, jellies, and quilts to feature, anyway.

You might be interested to know that I have stumbled upon a new source of material for a story that I am writing entitled "The Swap Shop." Every day at noon I listen to a public service program on a local radio station. People call in and tell about items they wish to buy, sell or trade. Yesterday, a Mr. Bowles called and reported that Aunt Mollie was successful in getting some speckled turkeys from someone in the county and that NOW he had a chicken incubator and brooder he wanted to sell or trade for anything liquid or solid -- except a dog. I'm checking into the reason a caller offered a size 8 wedding dress (unused) for sale, and several other interesting items. Incidentally, that's how I got my Hammond organ. A widow needed the money and I needed the organ. I really am playing at our little country church -- and the first Sunday I really did play too loud. Everyone said so! (I mentioned this in the ill-fated LETTER TO THE EDITOR.)

Thanks, a million.

Scatterbrained, but honest,
Lillian D. Champion

February 1974

First Person Editor
*Reader's Digest*
Pleasantville, New York 10570

Dear Mr. First Person Editor:

I am sending along, for your consideration, my latest brainstorm. This letter is not to tell you about my story (in less than ten minutes reading time, you will know all you need to know about it) but about ME. I'M A COMPULSIVE WRITER!

I've had a few things published (most of them locally) and I shudder every time I run across the ones I missed at my last burning.

I miss the excitement and activity of gathering material, especially since I've retired from my job as receptionist at my father's plumbing and electric company. The truth is: I didn't retire -- I was FIRED.

Housewives were calling for repairs on their pipes, ovens and corn poppers, and wanted rush jobs because they were expecting company or husbands returning from conventions -- or junior was in a program and the iron wouldn't get hot enough to press his pants.

One day I made a list of all the expected guests, the goers and comers convention wise, and the kids and their recital programs. It filled several pages. I mailed it to the State News Editor of THE ENQUIRER. He turned some of it over to the Society Section; some to the FEATURES, and the rest was used as news items. He even sent Doug Wallace and Charlie Black up to our town to take some pictures to use with the HOT news items.

Well, this tied up my father's phone and some of the customers got mad. My father was FURIOUS. Also, there developed some jealousy among the customers. Sometimes a drip call made the paper and the names mentioned during a call for major repairs got lost in the shuffle of notes. Business fell off. I don't even have references for another job.

I began to look for another source of news tips. My children stopped talking to me when they saw me following them with my pad and pencil. The friends they brought home from the university were instructed to remain silent if "Mama asks a lot of questions." One young man turned out to be the nephew of the Premier of Lebanon. He bought his first pair of blue jeans and learned to drive the tractor on our farm. That would have been a good story. It's too bad he had to be "incognito" at MY house.

The editor told me to write about things with which I was familiar. So, I wrote features about my neighbor's ceramics; another's jam, jellies and pickles -- and another's quilts. "There's gold in your own backyard," the editor said. So, I wrote about our dairy farm. ALL my stories were published -- in the SUNDAY MAGAZINE. Then one day the magazine editor told me, quietly, that they were about to run out of money. The State Editor had told him that when he asked me what I was writing FOR, that I replied "FOR MONEY."

Thus ended my career with the magazine. My husband was delighted. In seeking a cure for my compulsion, he is allowing me only one sheet of paper a day -- so that's why I'm writing on the back.

I haven't given up altogether. I've written my story, entitled FROM COWS TO CATFISH AND COLLARDS. It is a true story -- written Southern Fried Style (with TRUE GRITS -- and a little gravy). It tells about how we sold our dairy cows, built a lake and stocked it with catfish. I told it all in less than 2,500 words! I had to mail it way up north (to you) to keep from embarrassing my kin and the folks down at the Enquirer. I hope you are familiar with words like hushpuppies, collard greens, etc.

I have two other projects going to keep me busy, and away from writing. I am learning to play the organ and I am getting BRACES on my teeth. I am keeping a diary, however, for future stories. You see I am a GRANDMOTHER.

My only grandchild is, as the old saying goes, "Beautiful -- but mean as a snake." He was mean BEFORE HE WAS BORN, even. I was all set to go to Washington with the Pen Women (tea at the White House on April 17th) year before last. My grandchild was due April 1st. He didn't arrive 'til the 16th. I missed the tea.

When the doctor came out to tell us everything was fine and that it wouldn't be long, I took the opportunity to tell him that when he spanked the baby to give him an extra smack -- for ME. You know, that child still holds that against me. The other night on the phone (long-distance) I heard his mother say, "John, tell Grandmother, 'hello.'" Would you believe he reached down and unplugged the phone?

After reading this letter myself, I've decided that if you can't use my story, maybe you can use the letter -- or chop it up and pass it along to LAUGHTER or LIFE IN THESE UNITED STATES. I would rewrite it, and double-space it, but if I wait 'til tomorrow for more paper, I might just chicken out and not mail it.

Very hopefully yours,
Lillian D. Champion

### From Cows to Catfish and Collards

THE GOOD LORD MADE SIX TIMES AS MUCH WATER AS HE DID DRY LAND, SO -- AS ANY FOOL CAN PLAINLY SEE -- HE MEANT FOR MAN TO FISH SIX TIMES AS MUCH AS HE WORKS. This humorous notice appeared quite frequently on the office door of our small town's beloved fishing physician for more than 30 years. Everyone knew he was hopelessly hooked; and when he retired at 81, the whole county turned out to honor him with a new fishing boat and gear. He's gone now, but he left behind scores of West Central Georgians with the same hang-up.

For two years I have observed them -- not just men, but women and children -- at our farm catfish lake. They come in large number; sit beside the sometimes still water, and fervently hope that the bait is good, the line strong and the fish biting.

Most of our anglers are warm, lovable, really nice people, who seek a little relaxation and the thrill that comes with successfully landing a fish -- regardless of size. Many have become our close friends and have taught us some things we needed to know but never had time to learn.

My husband and I had never been fishing until we switched from cows to catfish. We operated a dairy for twenty-six years. After we built our lake, and opened it to all who pass our way, we discovered there is more to going fishing than catching fish. We have been pleasantly surprised at the fringe benefits.

Our switch from dairy cows to fish wasn't planned. It just happened. So did the collard patch. The 25 cents for seed, urged on us by our friendly garden-seed-man, has been our most profitable investment. I believe every seed came up, producing a superabundant crop of vegetables and another drawing card to our lake. We welcomed, with open arms, those who left rod and reel to assist in the garden behind the dam. In dry weather, they helped with plastic hose to siphon water to the wilting greens. We were amazed to discover how little we knew about raising vegetables. We were also amazed at the growing demand for our fish and our collards!

Dairying is a very demanding business. Regardless of weather, health or labor shortage, the cows must be milked twice a day. I remember the day my husband had several teeth extracted. He came home, took two aspirin, and milked 95 cows. We both looked forward to the day we could sleep 'til sunup, and could stay indoors and relax on a freezing cold or rainy day.

The beginning of the transition took place in the summer of 1970. We stood on the edge of a gully and watched as one of our near-ton-size cows was hoisted out by a wrecker. It was a Sunday afternoon. I guess you could say the ox was in the mire. Water had risen rapidly in the ditch blocked by the wedged Holstein. The cow died three days later from pneumonia.

Other cows had met a similar fate and we vowed to hire a dozier to fill the ditches. "Cows can swim -- build a lake instead," suggested someone in the small crowd that had gathered.

So, engineers came. They surveyed and drove stakes. They planned a 25-acre lake. It would cover the swamp and the ditches -- and a lot of our pasture. We cut it back to 18 acres. Someone should have told us THEN about catfish. Several small lakes would have been better.

Our daughter came home from her graduate school classes with the exciting news that her fiancé would accept his commission with the Army Veterinary Corps. She would hurry to complete her thesis and they would move their wedding date from September to mid-July. They wanted to go to Fort Richardson, Alaska! That dashed our hopes for a family cow-doctor within easy reach.

The week of the wedding, the lake was under construction. A short time later, we began to toy with the idea of selling the dairy herd and milking equipment. With both children educated, married, and on their own, we could slow down, take life a little easier. We mentioned our decision to a few friends. They told others. A few days later we made the sale.

On a morning in August, we marched more than a hundred cows down two miles of busy roads to another dairy farm. We were aided by the Highway Patrol and most of our community. "I've always wanted to help with a roundup," one neighbor commented. I followed the procession in our car. I couldn't walk. My left leg was in a cast. In the midst of the summer excitement, I tripped over something and broke my foot. I had an early start on our slowing-it-down-and-taking-it-easy plans.

One day a friend brought some literature on raising catfish. "That's it," we said. "We'll raise catfish and let people come and fish them out."

The rains came in November and filled the lake. We were ready for the fingerlings, but we had to wait 'til spring. The four-inch catfish arrived from the hatchery on April 15, 1971. There were 33,000 of them. They had to be fed every day for a whole year before they would be ready to be fished. As they grew, the daily amount of feed was increased.

One kind of pellet sinks and you never see the fish feeding. Another floats, and the top of the water comes alive with greedy fish. When people began to drop by at five in the afternoons, we threw out both kinds -- saving the floating pellets for the grand finale. We were making new friends and receiving offers of help from unexpected sources.

One afternoon, we told a neighbor that we hoped to build, someday, a modest cottage on the lake. Three days later, we heard from one of his friends -- a trust officer in a large bank in the city south of us. A lake property had been sold for a new development and there was a cottage that had to be moved or torn down. Would we be interested?

It was like a dream come true. We could have the pine-paneled cottage and its furnishings, along with the barbeque house and the boathouse, for practically nothing -- if we could move the whole works in three weeks. We located a professional house mover who even offered to take everything off our hands if we changed our minds.

We got it all moved without a hitch, and set to work putting a foundation under the cottage. When the mover called to inform us that he would come the next afternoon to let the house down on the foundation and retrieve his steel beams, we worked most of the night -- by car lights. We knew less about laying concrete blocks than we did about fishing. But we had enthusiasm. I crawled under the house, wearing my husband's coveralls, much too large for my small frame, and we started laughing. We laughed until we cried -- but we finished the pillars.

Surprisingly, the cottage rested fairly level on the foundation. We found a mason willing to help us rebuild the fireplace. We spent the winter refinishing the furniture and making repairs on the boathouse and barbeque hut. On Christmas Eve, we had a fire blazing in our fireplace, and two red socks hung from the mantle.

Shortly before our official opening, which was set for April (1972), we became furious when we discovered that night fishing was somebody's bag -- and it was OUR FISH in the bag that was being dragged across the dam. I donned the coveralls again and we patrolled the lake in the wee hours with a shotgun.

Opening day was to begin at seven-thirty, but our first fishermen arrived at dawn and pleaded with us to open the gate. The early worms got the fish; they caught 44 pounds (the fish averaged about a pound each) -- the largest catch for the day. They showed us in their Almanac where the 'signs' were right. We didn't know about 'signs.' We believed in pure luck. There was a buckeye in the cottage.

My husband and I were cleaning a two-pounder the day a big, jovial, super-fisherman showed up. Our fish was secured to a wood plank with a twenty-penny nail driven through the head. We were tugging at the tough skin with pliers. Big Ned (not his real name) produced his catfish skinners and a chop-axe and went to work teaching us how to clean fish. Then he offered to fry them. Amused, we let him. He not only cooked the fish, he made cornmeal hushpuppies and cole slaw. Everything was delicious.

We had guests often during the summer, and Ned did most of the cooking. He had grown up on the river where his family ran a fish camp. He was a gold mine of knowledge about fish and frying. He knew all about boats and gear, bait and bottle fishing, and running a trout line.

"Ned's been so miserable since he retired," his wife told us. "This is like an answer to a prayer." He was definitely the answer to ours.

A retired carpenter helped us screen the porch facing the lake. He had his rod set up only a few feet away and nine times one morning he had to lay his hammer down to reel in his fish. "Best job I ever had," he told us. He added another plank to our table on the porch, making room for 14 to eat in comfort.

"This cottage and all these volunteers -- how on earth did you do it?" one guest asked. I think it was the next day I found the second buckeye.

There is no gate fee at our lake. The only charge is for fish -- by the pound. There are rules and those who dare break them are not invited back. THOU SHALT NOT LITTER is our first rule. We don't allow drinking or bad language. One drunk, on being asked to leave, threatened to go to the newspapers. We dared him. We would have enjoyed the story.

Families come and bring picnic lunches. We watch fathers with small sons, and share their joy at a little boy's first catch. Older ones sit in chairs in the shade of the boathouse and reminisce with other veteran anglers. Some are in wheel chairs and one is blind. The younger fishermen stop by and offer assistance. Their voices and expressions soften. One lakeside romance was climaxed with a wedding. Our largest catch-of-the-season champion died. He had heart trouble, but fished until a few days before death claimed him.

Our fishing guests ply us with homemade cakes and cookies; jams, jellies and pickles. They bring plants, cuttings, and bulbs for our ever increasing-in-size flower beds. Two of the fishermen and their wives became 'lake-sitters,' making it possible for use to visit our daughter and her husband living happily in Alaska. We saw 60-pound cabbages near the state fish hatchers and went to the Silver

Salmon Derby at Seward. We saw some Holsteins. It was a busman's holiday.

The minister of a large church in a city not far from us brought his board of deacons and their wives to our lake one afternoon. The men caught, cleaned and fried the fish while their wives prepared the rest of the meal on the cottage porch. "You know, this is exactly what a lot of folks would like to have," I overhead someone say. "Yep -- it's pretty close to Heaven," replied another -- obviously as hopelessly hooked s our late physician. At any rate, we're glad we live in a place where people think a clean lake, a pine cottage, and an abundance of catfish and collards is 'good living.'

This should be the end of our story, but it's not quite finished yet. A portion of a proposed expressway, linking the two largest cities in our state, has been surveyed through our farm. At first, the center line of the limited access road was drawn on the aerial-photo-map right through the middle of our lake. Later, the stakes and red plastic ribbon markers were put out in our pasture, missing the lake by a few hundred yards to the West.

We have been swamped with offers from real estate agents, land dealers, and individuals. We set the price per acre so high that no one in their right mind would consider buying. One day the phone rang. "We're considering your price," a voice said. "Are you ready to sell?"

Our answer was, and still is, NO. We're going to wait. Because of the energy crisis, the expressway may not become a reality for several years. In the meantime, we'll keep our catfish and our collard patch -- and our faith in something bigger than buckeyes.

*Note by Mrs. Champion, 2008: The expressway was completed after I wrote this story. It diminished our farm*

*by nearly 40 acres, but we're keeping the farm, the lake and the cottage for our grandchildren.*

# The Chipley Historical Center

## Efforts to Restore Old City Hall Receive Strong Community Backing
*The Harris County Journal*, May 23, 1985

Plans for establishing the historical center in Pine Mountain moved rather slowly at first, but gained momentum during the latter part of 1984, according to Franklin Davenport, who spearheaded the project.

In 1982, the year of the Chipley - Pine Mountain centennial observance, Davenport obtained the promise of a $12,500 grant from the Callaway Foundation, Inc. When matching donated funds could not be raised by the first deadline, Davenport asked and received an extension of the deadline. Matching funds were still slow coming in, so a third and final deadline was extended to December 31, 1984. Matching funds had to come from contributors. The money could not be borrowed, according to terms of the grant.

The project really began to take shape when the Pine Mountain Kiwanis Club became interested when O.E. White, mayor at that time, made a talk to the club. He mentioned the project and the need for the matching funds. The club took on the project and, through auctions, barbecues and arts and crafts exhibits in Pine Mountain, raised $3,500.

In July 1984, Dr. Joseph Mahan, Historic Preservation Planner for the Lower Chattahoochee Area Planning and Development Commission, met with Davenport, Alf Mullins, James V. Edgar, mayor, and Lillian D. Champion in the mayor's office at the Pine Mountain City Hall.

The small group discussed with Mahan the need to restore the old City Hall and to obtain family histories and old records from churches, cemeteries, clubs and organizations. They decided on two points of action: (1) to mail out letters explaining the project to all residents of Pine Mountain and all rural route residents, and (2) to ask the Civilian Conservation Corps (CCC) organization, during their September meeting to be held at Roosevelt State Park here, for their support with both funds and materials to be put on display.

The letters were successful. By December 13th, a total of $10,000 had been turned in. That amount included the Kiwanis Club's $3,500 and a contribution of $1,000 from the CCC. The response from the CCC was from the entire organization and not from just the local members. Other contributions came from businesses, individuals, and organizations throughout the area.

During an organizational meeting held on December 13, Davenport was elected chairman and Lewis Bell vice-chairman of the project committee. Lillian Champion was elected secretary and publicity chairman, and Barbara Ewell, treasurer. Suggestions for a name for the project were made.

The publicity committee, through an article in The Harris County Journal, urged citizens to contribute the additional needed funds before the December 31st deadline. The goal was met and the Callaway Foundation, Inc., grant was obtained.

The Chipley Historical Center of Pine Mountain was the name selected by ballot at the second organizational meeting held on January 17, 1985. Dr. Mahan again met with the group and reported that he was applying for nomination of the Old City Hall to the National Register of Historic Buildings. He also suggested that committees be formed to begin working and planning various phases of the project.

The following committees were formed:

By-Laws: Lewis Bell, chairman; Bertha Ann Zachry, Annette Davis and Gerald Smith.

Publicity, Collection and Review Committee (charged with determining materials to be placed in the center: Lillian Champion, chairman; Angus Parker, Gerald Smith, Mary Askew, Winston Dunn, Mort Hoffman, and Ruth Gallops. Added later were Ken Askew, Gladys Roberts and Mary J. Thompson.

Building and Grounds: Franklin Davenport, chairman; Lewis Bell and Joseph Rupp.

Scrapbook Committee: Lucille Rupp and Annette Davis.

Furnishing Committee: Lucille Rupp, chairman; Annette Davis, Alice Mullins and Linda Straub (added later).

During the February meeting, it was decided to set a definite meeting date as the 4th Monday night of each month at 7 p.m. at City Hall. Also during that meeting, an estimate for re-plastering the old building was approved. All members attending through the February meeting were named to the Center's Board of Directors.

A set of by-laws was presented and approved at the March meeting. Plans for carpentry work, painting and wiring of the old building were approved with work to get underway at once. The building is to retain its original look with the ceiling and wainscoting of beaded boards.

At the April meeting, Davenport reported all plastering completed and carpentry work and wiring near completion. The painting will be finished in the very near future. The building will then be ready for display cabinets, file cabinets and other furnishings.

A sample membership card, drawn up by Mort Hoffman and Annette Davis was approved.

A finance committee, consisting of Annette Davis, Lewis Bell, Bertha Ann Zachry and Ken Askew, was approved at the April meeting.

A program committee, formed earlier and headed by Gerald and Sandra Smith, will present short programs on area history during Center meetings once the building restoration is completed and materials are on display.

The Center continues to accept contributions for promoting and maintaining the project. The tax-deductible contributions should be made to the Town of Pine Mountain. All donors names will be included in a plaque to be on display in the Center.

Meetings held at the City Hall on the 4th Monday of each month at 7 p.m. are open to the public.

## Historical Center to Open Sept. 15
*The Harris County Journal*, August 15, 1985

The ribbon-cutting ceremony for the opening of the Chipley Historical Center of Pine Mountain has been set for Sunday, September 15, at 3 p.m.

Committee members are busy preparing material for display and furnishing the recently restored old City Hall. The old building will serve as the town's historical center.

Among items contributed or loaned to the Center are books containing histories of the Goodman, Swint, Zachry, Hadley, Floyd, Marsh, and Huey families, and of other pioneer settlers of Harris County. Other books contain early census and marriage records of the area.

Additional family histories and records are being sought. Copies will be made at the Center of records for those wishing to retain originals. Contact Franklin Davenport, Lillian Champion, or Mrs. Joseph Rupp for information on house the Center will be open prior to September 15. Especially needed are Bible records of births, marriages, and deaths.

Among the interesting items to be on display at the Center are notes written to Chipley Mercantile Company (now Kimbrough's) in 1909. These notes bear the signatures of many of the early citizens of Chipley (now Pine Mountain) and reveal quite a bit of history of the early years of the town.

Some of the notes are as follows: "Let Earnest Sledge have a coffin for his baby, about $4.00 -- not over $5.00, a little robe ... a pair of shoes -- as cheap as you can. Charge to his account, but send me the bill." Oct 2, 1909. D. H. Satterwhite.

"Mr. Kimbrough, please send me by Ernest Sledge a pair of bed springs and andirons." Nov. 4, 1909. Mrs. D. H. Satterwhite. "I want nice andirons for the parlor."

"Mercantile Co., will you please let Armster Tucker have one bu. meal, 25 lb. sack flour, 6 lbs. lard, half-dollars sugar." July 24, 1909. Mrs. A. W. Babb.

Other notes requested lamp oil, wicks, 25-cent ties, 13-cent-a-pound meat, 5-cent hair pins and straight pins, farm tools, and other items.

One note requested Mr. Kimbrough to pay Dr. McLaughlin 75 cents for a tooth extraction and add the amount to a farmer's account at Chipley Mercantile.

Other notes were on sales slips printed with the names of other early business establishments -- Floyd and Hill, Pratt and Calhoun, C. G. Chambers (general merchandise and millinery), and stores operated by Strickland, Hopkins, and others.

From Birmingham, Alabama, came a story about how Mr. H. Hubert (Banks) Pratt, operator of a Chipley dry goods store, lost a leg while working on the railroad in Birmingham in December of 1885. The story also relates how Mr. Pratt's sister, Jimmie Lee, went to Birmingham to care for her brother. Pratt's roommate, McTyeire Harless, was quite smitten with Miss Pratt and wanted to marry her. She felt duty-bound to go back to Chipley to look after her aging mother and the wedding did not take place until January 28, 1911.

## Pine Mountain Military Monument

*The Harris County Journal*, June 15, 1989

As a fitting tribute during the week of Flag Day, the Pine Mountain Military Monument was dedicated Sunday afternoon across from the Post Office in Pine Mountain. The large bronze plaque contains the names of 533 names of veterans and persons currently in the military service who were raised in the vicinity of the Pine Mountain area. Names include those who served or are serving in any branch of the Armed Forces. A bronze star marks the names of those who died in service during the Civil War, World War I., World War II, Korea, and Vietnam. The project was begun more than a year ago by the Board of Directors of the Chipley Historical Center of Pine Mountain.

*Note by Mrs. Champion, 2008: Additional plaques have been added to the monument since the original dedication. In 2001, a plaque was added in memory of Marjorie Champion Salamone, daughter of Lillian and Hubert Champion, who died in the Pentagon on September 11, 2001. In 2007, another plaque was placed in memory of Jamie Bishop, son of Jeri and Michael Bishop. Jamie was a German teacher at Virginia Tech and was killed in the shooting rampage on that campus on April 16, 2007. Jamie grew up in his great-grandfather's (Dr. W. P. Ellis) former home in Pine Mountain.*

Made in the USA
Lexington, KY
09 December 2018